A SHORT
HISTORY OF
PHILOSOPHY

A SHORT HISTORY OF PHILOSOPHY

FROM ANCIENT GREECE TO THE POST-MODERNIST ERA

PETER GIBSON

This edition published in 2020 by Arcturus Publishing Limited
26/27 Bickels Yard, 151–153 Bermondsey Street,
London SE1 3HA

AD006852UK

Printed in the UK

CONTENTS

INTRODUCTION

This book gives an account of the philosophical ideas of the great European thinkers during the last two and half thousand years. Hence the book is a history of philosophy rather than a discussion of the lives of the famous philosophers, who occasionally became involved in great historical events or tried to make a mark on the public stage, but were mainly quiet scholars, little known during their day. However, in modern times, it is often claimed that you cannot understand a thinker without a good knowledge of the culture in which they lived, and the history of ideas has emerged as a discipline to support that view. It holds that to understand the progress of influential ideas we need to know about political power, technology, economics, religious practices, geography and social prejudices. The assumption of this work is that even though a particular culture clearly influences the thinkers it produces (no matter how objectively rational they try to be), philosophical ideas concern themes that arise in every human culture, and are of interest no matter who thought of them.

This book is an account of the main ideas of those considered to be the most important European thinkers in the subject – but how do we decide which thinkers are important? It is obvious that reputations rise and fall, but that usually happens during the first two centuries after the death of a philosopher, so the reputations of earlier Europeans are fairly settled. The status of a philosopher is usually judged by later thinkers who achieve the greatest respect in their own times. Sceptics may suspect a conspiracy, aimed to exclude 'undesirables', but wildly unorthodox accounts of philosophical history, though often interesting, are not usually well supported.

An obvious problem today is the place of women in the history of the subject. Modern scholars have shown that women have been much more involved in philosophy than was previously thought. In particular, they have been greatly engaged in philosophical discussions, especially in aristocratic courts where education levels were high, and in the salons of great cities such as Paris, where intellectuals gathered and debated. However, it remains true that significant influence in philosophy relies on books, rather than talk. Socrates did nothing but talk; his fame relies on Plato's written accounts of what he said. Women only moved to the forefront of philosophy when they gained entry to university education, beginning in the late nineteenth century, and when they were increasingly able to publish books. There are still problems of gender prejudice, but most modern philosophers judge ideas on their merits, not on the gender of the thinker.

If ideas are central to philosophy, then what is the importance of the history of the subject? The physical sciences and mathematics treat the history of their subjects as a side issue, mainly aimed at giving credit to earlier heroes. A good physicist, chemist or mathematician can ignore the history of their subject, if they wish, but the most important influence on any philosopher is the ideas of the leading thinkers of the immediately preceding generation, whether those ideas are accepted or rejected. A broad cultural history certainly throws light on philosophical ideas, but the greatest illumination comes from seeing how one philosophical idea leads to the next. Without some knowledge of the immediate influences it is hard to understand any great philosophical book. A determined reader can unravel the details of a complex text, and piece together the train of thought, but only the history can give an overview. Why was this book written? Which views does it aim to refute, without even mentioning them? Which well-known views does it try to reinforce? At the time of writing, which views were so well established that no one challenged them? How revolutionary is this book? For this reason the history of philosophy is viewed as a major part of its subject matter.

One reason for studying the history of philosophy is to address the controversial question of whether the subject makes progress. It is a well-known criticism offered by scientists that their subjects undoubtedly make remarkable progress, yet philosophers still seem to be arguing about the same problems that were debated two thousand years ago. Unlike scientists, philosophers rarely reach a consensus on anything, because every view that is proposed is immediately greeted with passionate objections, and most views are never fully confirmed or refuted.

Whether or not philosophy does make progress depends on what it aims to achieve. Take, for example, the theory known as Solipsism. A well-known train of thought begins with the fact that our knowledge of the world is based on our experiences of it, which are private to each person. If we only know our private experiences we can never be sure that they reveal an external reality. Maybe only the experiences exist. Maybe other people also don't exist, except as one individual's personal experiences. It therefore seems possible that nothing exists at all, apart from that person's private mental world. There have been a few attempts to refute solipsism, usually by pointing to features of this very private world which seem impossible if nothing exists beyond it, such as the person's concept of God, or their language, or the consistency of their experiences, or unexpected and unwanted events, but none of them seem strong enough to prove the point. We are left with solipsism as a possibility. We can't even dismiss it as a remote possibility, because it is unclear how to assess its remoteness.

Nobody, however, believes this theory, because it is a dead end for all enquiry, and it implies that all experiences are delusions, and life is therefore pointless. But if it is a dead end and no one believes the conclusion, why bother with it? There is a horrible inevitability about the train of thought that leads to solipsism, so the only way to avoid it is to refuse to ask the first question. If someone asks you how you know there is a world outside your mind, just walk away, or change the subject! But if we refuse to ask questions which might lead to unwelcome conclusions, that sounds like the end of human intellectual activity. 'We must follow the wind of the argument, wherever it leads,' said Plato, and that is the spirit of philosophy. If the arguments lead to dead ends, or hopeless puzzles, or go round in circles, or reach two equally implausible but contradictory conclusions, then thinkers just have to live with that, given that not thinking at all is the only alternative.

Solipsism is a familiar and permanent landmark on our intellectual map, and its discovery (which most clearly emerged when people pondered Descartes' famous 'I think, therefore I am') was an achievement of philosophy. The history of philosophy is the story of how rational trains of thought were pursued, gradually revealing a huge map of possible reasoning about the human situation. This process of mapping started with a few simple problems, and theories intended to answer them. The map is now a huge and intricate network of pathways and landmarks, still containing areas where the details are vague, or entirely obscure.

So if we abandoned Western philosophy and started all over again, would the same map emerge? It would be naïve to think so, because the enquiry is partly guided by prejudices, shared delusions, the influences of particular languages and factors such as technology and styles of thinking. But the subject matter – the problems of human existence – remains the same, and the way people reason differs very little in books written far away and long ago. It would be surprising if the new map didn't have a lot in common with the old one, and it would certainly be disappointing if no one had noticed the problem of solipsism.

The main aim of the following accounts of the ideas of the great thinkers is to place them next to their immediate predecessors, to show how one scheme of thought grows from another. Before starting, though, it will be helpful to have a short overview of the whole two and a half thousand years of shared effort. There are some wider patterns to be seen, and occasional major shifts in thought.

A HISTORICAL OVERVIEW

580–400 BCE Philosophy began when early thinkers searched for the simplest principles which lie behind nature. Their approach was revolutionary because they wanted answers that were part of nature, not part of human religion or mythology. Their work would now be described as theoretical science, and it was based on observation, but it was their method which led to philosophy. Their theories were not only imaginative but were supported by reasons for each belief, and disagreements with, and criticisms of, the reasons were welcomed rather than rejected. The dialectical method of discussion emerged, which follows proposals, objections and counter-objections, often illustrating principles with precise examples. Socrates made successful definition the target of the discussions, and he expanded the subject matter to include morality.

400–100 BCE Most of the early writings were lost, so philosophy became a major subject with the surviving works of Plato (c.427– 347 BCE), followed by Aristotle (384–322 BCE). Plato expanded the subject even further, to include politics, language and the mind, to which Aristotle added logic. Both of them wrote lengthy and systematic works, and founded schools to teach their ideas. In the next century further schools appeared in Athens, notably those of the Epicureans and the Stoics. Schools teaching scepticism and anarchic lifestyles also arose, and opponents of philosophy said the art of persuasion should replace the pointless pursuit of truth.

100 BCE**–600** CE This vigorous rational Greek culture was gradually restricted by the rise of the Roman Empire, though most educated

Romans followed either the Epicureans or the Stoics. During this period the belief that there was just one supreme God gradually replaced belief in the 12 gods on Mount Olympus, and this monotheistic view became less tolerant of open philosophical debate, because most questions were settled by knowledge of God's will, rather than by human reason. After Christianity took over the empire, philosophy was squeezed out, and after a thousand years the schools were closed.

1090–1350 When, after an interval of several unphilosophical centuries, there was a revival of interest in reading books (especially those of Aristotle), it was the writings of Augustine of Hippo which saved philosophy, because he had insisted that thoughtful Christians must address the questions raised by pagan philosophers. Hence there followed two of the liveliest centuries in the history of philosophy, when the new universities were full of careful analysis and public disputes. All the thinkers agreed on the basic doctrines of Christianity, but other opinions differed widely, with some (such as Aquinas) emerging as heroes, and others (such as William of Ockham) facing persecution.

1400–1650 This wave of enthusiasm for disputes was once again suppressed, and another two centuries passed with little philosophical activity. This all changed during the Renaissance, with philosophy emerging towards the end of that period. This coincided with the development of the new sciences, and was again the achievement of one individual, in this case René Descartes, who insisted that science needed support from metaphysics at a time when many scientists just wanted to get on with the experiments. At the same time Hugo Grotius pushed moral thinking away from ancient virtues and towards legalistic rules for performing right actions.

1650–1800 Philosophy was very active during the period we call the Enlightenment, with printed books widely distributed and universities growing in importance. Every thinker responded to the growing success of science, and their approaches can be labelled as either rationalist or empiricist. Spinoza and Leibniz show the huge confidence in reason which was typical of the time, whereas Locke, Berkeley and Hume took the more cautious empiricist approach (which depends on experience). At the end of the period Immanuel Kant dramatically turned the debate inwards, and focused on how our minds work, rather than on our knowledge of the world.

1800–1830 The emergence of revolutionary politics in France, and romanticism in literature, brought the Enlightenment to an abrupt end. In Germany philosophers inspired by Kant turned to idealism, which says our mental life *is* our reality, and Hegel became the leading thinker of the period, which in turn provoked Karl Marx to produce an influential political theory. The rights of women became an issue, and moral rules were said to promote either duty or pleasure.

1830–1890 As romantic enthusiasm died down, several very independent thinkers produced rebellious views. Both Schopenhauer and Kierkegaard disliked Hegel's lectures, with Kierkegaard launching the very individualistic view which became

Existentialism. Nietzsche attacked conventional and Christian beliefs, and explored the development of new personal values. Peirce, on the other hand, made practicality the aim of thought, and science its basis, which thus launched Pragmatism.

1880–1939 The next generation of philosophers learned new techniques of logic from mathematicians, and started modern Analytic philosophy, which focused on precise arguments and the analysis of language. Frege made the first steps, then Russell and Wittgenstein developed the approach, with the Viennese Logical Positivists turning it into a tough empirical and scientific view which aimed to entirely abandon metaphysics. The techniques of precise definition and logic were then used to discuss ethics and religion, which usually led to fairly sceptical views.

1900–1945 In Germany, Edmund Husserl began the approach known as phenomenology, which aimed at exact and neutral accounts of conscious experience. The objective findings of science were largely ignored, in favour of trying to think more clearly about the subjective truths of being a human being. Henri Bergson explored the role of memory and time in our inner lives, and Martin Heidegger moved this approach towards Existentialism, in which our reality is created by the process of daily decision-making and interaction with the world. Jean-Paul Sartre made Existentialism much clearer, and the idea that we can remake ourselves through choices turned into a popular movement.

1945– Philosophy now divided into two very different approaches (known as Analytic and Continental). The Analytic school, led by logicians, dominated most universities in the English-speaking world, while the Continental school, led by individualists with political commitments and a desire for liberation, flourished in France, especially with a series of books that appeared in the 1960s. New areas were opened up. Analytic philosophers turned their attention to the nature of the mind, and their ethical thinking became more practical (by attending to medical ethics, for example). Metaphysics was revived, and ancient virtue theory, which focused on qualities of character rather than on right and wrong actions, gained many followers. In France, the great influences were Husserl, Heidegger, Marx and Freud, and the gap between philosophy and cultural studies almost disappeared.

CHAPTER 1

THE PHILOSOPHY OF NATURE (585–399 BCE)

The earliest period of philosophy was dominated by famous individuals, who were treated more like high priests of knowledge than as humble students of the truth. At first each thinker simply proposed his own theory of nature's hidden secrets. Proper philosophy began when it was realized that these basic theories have many implications, and when the thinkers responded to criticism with cool arguments rather than hostility. There is an interval of nearly two hundred years between the earliest ideas and the writing of the first surviving books. Philosophy began very slowly, but we can see a mounting sense of excitement among the Greeks towards the end of this first period, as the discussions become more complex, intense and wide-ranging.

EXPLAINING NATURE (585–420 BCE)

The ancient Greeks were in agreement about two facts regarding the origin of philosophy: that it began in Miletus, a wealthy

Greek colony on the coast of modern Turkey, and that the first philosopher was Thales, who flourished around 585 BCE. Two further citizens of Miletus – Anaximander (fl. 570 BCE) and Anaximenes (fl. 550 BCE) – extended the thinking of Thales, and launched the philosophical tradition.

ΘΑΛΕΣ

Above: Thales was the earliest philosopher, and tried to deduce the simplest hidden principles of nature.

Thales was a distinguished thinker in many areas, including geometry and astronomy, and was later named as the first of the Seven Sages of Greece. Aristotle tells us that Thales was so struck with the remarkable properties of magnets that he thought there might be a soul in all of nature, and that this soul was the cause of movement. His most celebrated proposal was that the first principle of nature is water – that is, all explanations of nature lead back to water, as the fundamental substance which gives rise to everything else. Presumably this idea arose because of the universal presence of moisture, not only in the seas and in rain, but also within plants and animals, and in the underground sources of rivers. Thales even suggested that the known world floats on water.

This isolated theory is important because it provoked disagreement and rival theories, and suggested new problems. Thales found nature puzzling, and was not interested in explanations involving angry gods or local spirits. He did not reject Greek mythology, but he looked for an explanation of nature within nature itself – one which could be understood by mere human reason.

Thales' theory is, of course, the beginning of science, rather than of philosophy, but for two thousand years they formed a single subject. The interest for philosophers was to follow the scientific theory that nature is essentially water, and see where it led. Anaximander belonged to the next generation in Miletus, and must have known Thales well, but he rejected water as the first principle (since, for a start, it can't explain dry things). The very idea that he could reject the theory of the person who probably taught him is a striking development, since the acceptance of orthodox beliefs had always been the norm. The critical attitude needed for philosophy was beginning to emerge.

Anaximander presumed that we are at the centre of the cosmos, and he concluded that the cosmos must be eternal. He thought in terms of a continual process of creation and destruction guided by justice, since most ancient Greeks saw the cosmos as the embodiment of moral goodness. His most famous idea is that the process of creation and destruction can be explained by a single underlying substance, which is not something we know (such as water), but is the *apeiron* ('the unlimited'), which is eternal and boundless, and can take many forms. This bold speculation still appeals to modern physicists who seek a unified account of matter.

Anaximenes, who must have known Anaximander, was also interested in astronomy and the foundations of nature. He evidently disliked the obscure concept of the *apeiron*, because he looked for a basic substance that is observable, and decided that air is a better candidate than water, because air condenses into water, and water evaporates back into air. Nature depends on continual change, and these transformations of air can actually be observed. He was particularly struck by human breath (pneuma), which shows the total dependence of humans on air.

The Milesian school ended when the Persians conquered the city. However, the important contribution of these thinkers is not only their ideas, but the fact that Anaximander and Anaximenes wrote books about them. Their books were copied and circulated, so subsequent generations were no longer starting their enquiries from a blank slate. Maybe the real stars of this history are not the thinkers, but their books.

The next major thinker about nature was startlingly different. Pythagoras (fl. 530 BCE) came from the island of Samos, not far from Miletus. He quickly became a legendary figure, credited with many achievements which may not all have been his. Since a Pythagorean school emerged from his career, and lasted for at least nine hundred years, we know quite a lot about his doctrines. He took the main feature of the cosmos to be its beautiful harmonious order, rather than its cycle of creation and destruction. Therefore music had a special status for him, because of its harmony, and this led to an intriguing discovery. If you stretch a string and twang it, you can produce two pairs of notes which exhibit very harmonious intervals. Stopping the string at exactly half of its length results in the note going up an octave. If your stop reduces the vibrating length by two fifths, the note goes up by a fifth. This is hugely important for musical harmony, but the interest of Pythagoras was in the exact numbers involved. It appeared that harmony could be explained by numbers, suggesting that nature might be explained by its ratios.

If perfect ratios, such as 2:1 for the octave and 3:2 for the fifth, could explain harmony, then the hunt was on for other ratios in nature. Pythagoras attracted followers, and set up a school at Croton in southern Italy. The scholars developed mystical doctrines, many of them centred on patterns of numbers, such as the tectractys (a four-row triangle, with four, three, two and one units in the rows), which seemed to symbolize the structure of nature. The doctrines developed by the highly secretive Pythagoreans led to increasingly sweeping claims, amounting to the idea that nature is literally *made* of numbers. This can be illustrated by the later idea of the Golden Ratio (where a line is divided into larger **a** and smaller **b**, so that the ratio of **a** to **b** is identical to the ratio of the whole line (**a** +**b**) to **a** (that is, a:b = (a+b):a). This ratio (roughly 1.61:1) was felt to exhibit visual harmony, just as the earlier ratios exhibited audible harmony.

Initially Pythagoras' idea that nature is mathematical may have held limited interest for philosophers, but a dramatic discovery soon changed that. The Pythagoreans saw nature as entirely controlled by the harmonious ratios of whole numbers. It is not surprising that they found a mystical significance in the whole numbers, and even understood moral justice in terms of ratios. The bombshell that disrupted this neat view was a new proof, showing that the diagonal of a unit-sided square cannot be expressed as a ratio of whole numbers (because it is the square root of two, which is an 'irrational' number). The Pythagoreans had to face the failure of their precise and complete theory of nature. (The modern logician Kurt Gödel had a similar impact in 1931, when he showed that some truths of arithmetic can never be proved). After this event the status of mathematics became a major and enduring topic in philosophy.

Ephesus was a coastal city near Miletus, and the fascinating figure of Heraclitus flourished there in around 490 BCE. We have more than a hundred of his short quotations, which include ideas on nature, knowledge, morality and politics. He was clearly influenced by the Milesians, because he proposed that the first principle of nature is fire. This plays the same role as the *apeiron* of Anaximander, by keeping nature eternally the same, despite its superficial changes. Fire also has the same advantage as water or air, in that we can actually observe it, and assess its qualities. Heraclitus' concept is close to the crucial role played by energy in modern physics.

Pythagoras was impressed by order, but Heraclitus was far more taken by nature's changes and instability. His most famous remark is 'all is flux' (or 'everything flows'), which introduces the idea that nature is dominated by unstable Becoming rather than stable Being. His famous illustration of this idea is that 'you cannot step twice into the same river', which implies that even stable elements such as rivers are in a continual shifting process, just as fire is both eternal and constantly changing. The stability that we find in much of nature, despite the underlying fiery flux, is illustrated by pairs of opposing forces that achieve equilibrium, such as the tensions found in a lyre or a bow. New things also emerge from the 'strife' between opposites, so this energetic tension is the driving force of nature.

HERACLYTUS

Above: Heraclitus saw nature as continually changing, with tensions between opposed forces producing stability.

An important step was Heraclitus' focus on the word *logos*, which roughly means rational speech, and is the hallmark of clear thought and successful explanation. This began the idea that philosophy aspires to calm and accurate reasoning, even when surrounded by chaos, and shows it becoming more self-conscious about its own activities. Heraclitus was doubtful about our ability to achieve *logos*, though, and he gloomily remarked that 'the fairest cosmos is just a random heap of sweepings'. Of human behaviour he made the striking remark that 'character is fate'.

The early Greek world was spread widely across the Mediterranean, and the next important figure, Parmenides, emerged in Elea, which was on the west coast of Italy, where he probably flourished around 470 BCE. He is a figure of major importance, because he asked new deep questions which inspired both awe and perplexity, offered arguments to support each part of his position, and was probably the first philosopher to study what we now call metaphysics. His quotations are confined to the fragments of his only piece of writing, a poem about nature.

Rather than explaining nature by an observable element or by mathematics, he aimed to directly understand existence itself, covered by the word 'Being'. This may look like a hopeless task, but it has often fascinated philosophers, and it resurfaced in the nineteenth-century philosophy of Hegel. Parmenides said we begin to understand Being through its contrast with Non-Being. He raised the question of what happens when you continually subdivide physical matter, and concluded that you would eventually subdivide it out of existence, which is an absurdity. Hence dividing matter is impossible, and Being is a perfect unity. Also, all movement needs an emptiness into which it can move, but emptiness is Non-Being and cannot exist, so the apparent movement of Being must be an illusion (and even the Becoming of Heraclitus never occurs). Since, also, no power could produce Being out of Non-Being, or reduce Being back to Non-Being, it follows that Being must be eternal. Finally, there is no reason why it should be greater in one direction rather than another, so true reality must be spherical in shape.

The startling conclusion of these very abstract arguments is that Being is actually an eternal, indivisible, unmoving sphere (later called 'the One'). It led to heated subsequent discussion, and found few followers, but what fascinated philosophers were the careful arguments offered by Parmenides in support of his views. His underlying principle that things can only be different if there is some reason for the difference came to be called the Principle of Sufficient Reason – that there is a reason (or explanation or cause) for everything. Because Parmenides favoured the implications of his reasoning, rather than the observations of his senses (which show movement, for example) he is seen as the first Rationalist philosopher (as opposed to the Empiricists, who favoured experience). He also focused later discussions on change, divisibility, the unity of nature, what is necessarily true, and non-existence.

Parmenides' reasoning about the impossibility of movement was endorsed in further arguments created by his younger follower, Zeno of Elea. The most famous of these is The Achilles, which asks whether the great athlete Achilles could overtake a tortoise in a race, if the tortoise started ahead of Achilles. Common sense says yes, but try reasoning about it as follows: if Achilles is going to overtake the moving tortoise, then clearly Achilles must first reach the current location of the tortoise; when Achilles reaches that location, clearly the moving tortoise will not be there, because it will have moved on; Achilles must thus repeat the operation (of getting to the new location of the tortoise), but the same thing will necessarily happen again; this has to occur every time Achilles tries to catch the tortoise. Hence reason shows that Achilles can never chase and overtake a moving tortoise. This means our normal experience of movement must be a delusion, and Parmenides was right that movement does not occur. If (like most people) you don't accept Zeno's conclusion, it is not enough to cite common sense about races – you must specify what is wrong with his argument (which focuses on infinitely small intervals of space and time).

The next major explorer of nature, Empedocles, flourished in Akragas, in southern Sicily, in about 455 BCE. His most famous proposal is that rather than one first principle of nature there are four: earth, air, fire and water. He could see no reason to give any one of these priority, but each of them is simple and pure, and they are found in everything which exists. Familiar substances are explained by combinations of these four elements, so that blood is equal parts of each, and bone is two parts each of water and earth, and four parts fire. His basic theory was endorsed by Aristotle, and endured for the next two thousand years.

Empedocles believed the cosmos is eternal, but it was originally very different, consisting of a single divine entity, united by the power of love. The impact of hate dissolved this unity, and the cosmos we experience, with its four elements, is a continual process of combination (caused by love) and division (caused by hate). The living creatures we see now are the result of the elimination of more chaotic and unsuccessful creatures (implying a one-off burst of Darwinian natural selection). Empedocles was also interested in the mind and perception, and made the interesting remark that we have two eyes, but see only one world.

Another individualistic approach to the nature of matter was developed by Anaxagoras (fl. 460 BCE), who felt that the four elements needed a deeper explanation. The idea that the complexity of nature can be reduced to a tiny number of principles seemed unlikely (and he certainly disliked the One of Parmenides), so he saw no limit to the range of basic facts. He distinguished between substances which are pure, and remain the same when you divide them (as when dividing water reveals more water), and those which are made of parts which are different (as when a beach is made of pebbles, rather than of more 'beach'). But he was particularly struck by the nature of seeds, which seem pure, and yet produce plants and animals of huge complexity. The multitude of these pure substances were his foundations, and the important four elements are combinations of these substances.

This idea did not catch on, but his idea that nature is guided by intelligence was very influential. The order of nature is amazing, but it seemed that only minds could produce order, and minds are pure, self-controlled and the source of causes. Hence mind is at the heart of nature, which moved towards a more modern view of religion, and made the nature of mind a key topic for philosophers. His religion certainly wasn't conventional, because he was charged with impiety for saying that the Sun (which was assumed to be a god) was merely a lump of stone. It is significant that Anaxagoras lived in Athens, which was becoming the new home of philosophical thought.

Belief that elements explain nature was becoming the settled view, but it was not the last word on the subject. Democritus (fl. 420 BCE) came from Abdera, a Greek colony on the Black Sea, and developed a quite different explanation. The theories involving elements explained the variety of nature by their different combinations or transformations, but no further explanation could be given of the elements themselves. The new theory (developed by Leucippus and Democritus) dug deeper, seeing combinations as the key to understanding natural things, but proposing extremely small 'atoms' as the ingredients. These indivisible atoms are too small to see, infinite in number, and have unlimited shapes and sizes. They connect to one another in many ways, such as by hooks or plugs, and the qualities of large objects result from whether their atoms are securely linked, or are smooth, lumpy or spiky. Democritus was an empiricist (relying on experience), and assumed that the movements we see in nature are real. But a crowded infinity of atoms needs some space if they are to move, so he proposed the existence of a perfect 'void' between the atoms. This obviously defied the claim of Parmenides that such Non-Being is impossible.

Democritus also wrote about the possibilities of knowledge. Although an empiricist, he was sceptical about the senses, because we and animals experience the same reality in many different and contradictory ways. Sense experience of qualities also did not fit his atomic theory, because we experience things as hot or cold or coloured, but 'reality is atoms and void'. Since this reality is too small for us to see, 'truth is hidden in an abyss'.

Many isolated sayings about morality were later attributed to Democritus, but he seems to have been the most purely scientific of the early thinkers. His atomic theory was, however, highly significant in pure philosophy, for two reasons. The idea that absolutely everything is atoms and void seems fine for rocks and earth, a bit perplexing for living plants, and rather alarming when applied to human beings. In particular, it means that our minds are purely physical, and thought is just atomic movement, which is the first 'physicalist' theory of the mind. Secondly, since no mind is involved in the drifting and connection of the atoms, this is the first suggestion that we are not

Above: In Athens, Democritus (centre) said that reality is just atoms and void; Protagoras (right) said there are no facts about reality, just opinions.

in charge of our own thoughts. This view would later be called 'determinism', which is the denial that we have free will, or full control of our own choices.

PERSUADERS (450–420 BCE)

By 450 BCE philosophy was becoming a well-defined subject, based in Athens, which had become a democracy, ruled directly by an assembly of citizens, and was entering its golden age. The law courts were also very active, and citizens regularly had to stand up and defend their rights. This needed a new skill – public speaking – and there was a big demand for anyone who could teach the skills of successful persuasion. Philosophers, who studied arguments, were experts in this skill, but there was a problem. Was the aim of public argument to arrive at the truth, or to win? Most citizens preferred to win, and new teachers appeared (referred to, sarcastically, as the 'sophists', the wise men) who could teach them to do it. These Sophists not only took less interest in truth, but also developed arguments to show why truth is overrated, thus expanding new sceptical areas of philosophy.

Gorgias (483–375 BCE), who came from Leontini in Sicily, travelled widely – including to Athens – giving public demonstrations of oratory and charging pupils for lessons. He is best remembered for one argument (probably aimed at the claims of Parmenides about Being), which proves conclusively that absolutely nothing exists!

1) There is only Being or Non-Being, and Non-Being doesn't exist.
2) Being is everlasting or created, or both.
3) Everlasting Being can't exist, because it is boundless and so has no position.
4) Being can't be created from Being, nor from Non-Being, so it can't be created.
5) Being can't be both, because that is a contradiction.
6) Being can't be One, because anything with size is divisible, and it can't be Many, because that is made of Ones, which don't exist. So nothing exists.

If that isn't enough, he also adds that thought can never grasp true Being, and that our perception of Being could never be communicated.

We must presume that Gorgias did not believe his own conclusion, but it reveals a lot about Athenian philosophers. They were so intoxicated with arguments that opponents began to make fun of them. At a later date Athenian philosophers would pay significant sums of money to buy good arguments, the way we might buy a painting. Gorgias may have been joking, but the argument is clever, and, like The Achilles, offers a serious challenge. What is wrong with it? Can we *prove* that we know what exists?

The challenge became clearer when Protagoras of Abdera (c.490–c.420 BCE) boldly proclaimed that 'Man is the measure of all things', by which he meant that everything that seems to be known depends entirely on the viewpoint of the knower, which constantly varies. He thus committed himself to the doctrine of Relativism, which, in its strongest form, entirely rejects the idea that anything is 'true'. Hence all that matters is rhetoric, which is the skilled art of persuasion.

These views led to the long-running *nomos-physis* debate (where *nomos* is convention or law, and *physis* is nature). Relativism implies that the moral virtues are not natural truths about human life, but mere conventions invented by us. The debate concerned first whether virtue actually is unnatural, and then whether conventions improve nature or undermine it. Protagoras was criticized for being able to make 'the weaker argument appear to be the stronger', and his most influential claim was that for every argument that can be proposed, there is always an equally good argument on the other side, so they always cancel out. This eventually led to Scepticism becoming a well-supported school of philosophy. Interest in the Sophists has increased in modern times, because Relativism has become a major issue in modern culture.

SOCRATES (470–399 BCE)

Although he wrote nothing, Socrates was probably the most influential of all philosophers. He was an Athenian who started his career studying explanations of nature, and is said to have met the elderly Parmenides. He then changed his field of interest, probably in reaction against the devaluing of truth and of agreed virtues by the Sophists. He became one of the most famous citizens of Athens, but in old age he was dramatically charged with impiety and corrupting the young, and was executed by means of being compelled to drink a cup of hemlock. He could have escaped, but preferred to submit to the law. If philosophy has a saint and martyr, it is Socrates.

Unusually, his character and life had as much influence as

Above: The strongest character in early philosophy was Socrates, whose challenging and inventive conversations were carefully recorded.

his specific teachings. Rather than the study of nature, his new interest was in the question 'How should people live their lives?' He pursued this topic by continual conversations in public places, with an audience of passing citizens. What they heard was a process called the *elenchus*, which was a gentle interrogation of people who held strong views, to see if these were consistent, accurate, clear and justified. The conversations were conducted by a man who liked to tease, who would sometimes play devil's advocate, who regularly admitted that he was ignorant, and who delighted in being proved wrong; his aim was to achieve agreement rather than to impose his own views. His whole career was a masterclass in rational conversation.

Socrates introduced definition as a new target in philosophy, implying that the clarity of our concepts is the key to wisdom. The conversations broke concepts into components, grouping them into categories aimed at summarizing their essential natures. His view was that the unexamined life was not worth living, so his examinations aimed at improving character by clearly defining the necessary virtues. He was the first to focus on *eudaimonia* as the aim of human life. This is traditionally translated as 'happiness', but it is more like success in life than a mere cheerful feeling, and 'flourishing' seems the best translation.

It was clear to Socrates that a flourishing individual is a virtuous individual, meaning they have an excellent disposition and their behaviour is equally worthy. The best people perform deeds which can be described as 'fine', or even 'beautiful'. Apart from trying to define the virtues, two problems bothered him: whether we can teach people to be virtuous, and whether the virtues are unified, so that they could all be achieved in a co-ordinated way.

It is easier to teach virtues if they are conventional (*nomos*) than if they are natural (*physis*), so the ideal is to develop conventions which are in tune with nature.

For Socrates, the unifying ingredient of the virtues is reason. He was struck by the problem of *akrasia* (lack of control), which is the puzzle of why people do things they know are bad for them (such as smoking). The common view is that it is simply weakness, because emotional desire overcomes common sense, but Socrates disagreed. He took the mind (*psuchē*, often translated as 'soul') to be the essence of a person, and this is wholly unified, rather than in conflict, and is controlled by reason. Therefore all foolish decisions result from ignorance, and a modern person who smokes must either intend to die young, or believe that the evidence about cancer is false, rather than having a weak will. This 'intellectualist' view of Socrates applied to all of the virtues, so that courage, for example, is more concerned with judging when to confront danger, rather than with a mere endurance of pain or death. The traditional Greek slogan for virtue was 'benefit your friends, and harm your enemies', but Socrates was in the forefront of a new movement which said that only the law (not the private individual) should take vengeance, and he urged us to befriend our enemies, and not return evil for evil.

PHILOSOPHICAL SYSTEMS (399–322 BCE)

At this point in our history everything changes, because a large collection of books by Plato and Aristotle has survived. In neither case do we have their complete works, because the specialist works of Plato are lost, as are the popular dialogues of Aristotle, but their surviving works form two fat volumes which are the real basis of Western philosophy. Their additional interest is that Plato was the pupil of Socrates, and Aristotle was the pupil of Plato, and in each case the pupil both revered and rebelled against his teacher.

PLATO (428–347 BCE)

The first response Plato made to the execution of Socrates was to record the powerful conversations of his teacher, so he began to produce wonderfully well-written dialogues, each one focused on an attempt to define an important concept. Those that are assumed to be the earliest ones simply recorded the ideas of Socrates, but Plato was a great philosopher himself, with his own theories. In later dialogues he attributed to his teacher some theories with which the older man might have disagreed. It is hard to disentangle the two thinkers in the texts.

Plato acquired followers, and in around 387 BCE he founded his Academy in Athens, which may have been the world's first university. Standards were high, a good knowledge of geometry was a minimum requirement, and many subjects were studied. Plato spent most of his life in the Academy, in retirement from public life, though later in his career he travelled to Sicily, to advise the rulers of Syracuse (a venture which seems to have gone badly).

Above: Plato's Academy in Athens was a school of mathematics and philosophy, where day-long arguments were a way of life.

It has famously been observed (with some truth) that all of Western philosophy is simply footnotes to Plato. Nearly all the topics of modern philosophy are mentioned in his writings, and many are explored in great detail. We can see that this is so if we describe his ideas using the modern subject headings, beginning with the area for which he is most famous – metaphysics.

Plato preferred to see the world in terms of the enduring Being of Parmenides, rather than the process of Becoming favoured by

Heraclitus. However, sense experience shows the shifting world of Becoming, and only reason can reveal the nature of Being. Some things are more real than others, and he describes an ascending reality which starts with mere shadows and reflections, then rises to the objects of sense experience, then to the principles of reality (such as mathematics), and only attains the highest reality in the world of pure ideas (known as the 'Forms'). The Forms are the eternal and unchanging blueprints of reality. For example, the world contains innumerable horses (past, present and future), which all share the essential features which constitute a horse. Such regularity in nature can only be controlled and explained by the Form of the horse, which is a pure and general idea. Plato's Forms are a suggestion for the foundations of nature, as rivals to earlier ideas of water or mathematics or four elements.

PLATO ARISTONIS F. ATHENIENSIS
Ex marmore antiquo

Above: Most of the popular works of Plato survive, containing his idealist view of reality and a devotion to virtue.

The famous analogy of the Cave (in his dialogue *Republic*) illustrates the levels of reality. Human life is like slaves chained in a cave, endlessly watching shadows of objects cast on a wall, and thinking the shadows are real because that is all they ever see. The most thoughtful slaves (the philosophers) work out the truth, find the source of the shadows, and eventually emerge into the sunlight of true reality. Plato never denies the reality of the world we normally experience, and remarks that our descriptions of the physical world should aim to 'cut nature at the joints' – that is, accurately respond to the facts. But Plato was a rationalist philosopher, and aimed to understand the Forms by sustained and careful reasoning, based on the critical approach developed by Socrates. This rational procedure is called 'dialectic' – sympathetic critical discussion between two people, which gradually edges towards the truth.

In his later dialogues Plato confronts two problems for the theory of Forms. The first is the relationship between the form of the horse and an individual horse. A real horse has distinctive features, such as its particular colour, but it 'partakes' of the Form because it is like other horses. But partaking is between two very different things – a pure idea and a physical animal – so this relationship remains unclear. The other problem is that we recognize a particular horse because it is like the general idea that we have of a horse; but if recognition is spotting a resemblance, how do we recognize the *Form* of the horse? What does *that* resemble? It would be absurd to invent a 'super-Form', simply to clarify what it is we are thinking about. Plato hit a familiar problem in metaphysics – how does this process ever get started? At some point we have to simply recognize *something*.

Plato explored Epistemology (the theory of knowledge) in his dialogue *Theaetetus*. In trying to define knowledge, it is clear that a person needs to believe something, and what they believe must be true, but that is not enough because it could involve luck (like a blind person who happens to be on the right road, he says). The further requirement is *logos*, the concept highlighted by Heraclitus that you must be able to give a rational account of *why* it is believed. In modern times this has become the idea that knowledge might be 'true justified belief' (which has led to heated discussion). Plato also believed that we have innate ideas as a source of knowledge, which are available to reason rather than experience. His famous illustration in the dialogue *Meno* is the interrogation of an apparently ignorant slave boy on the subject of geometry. Although he has never studied it, the boy can give sensible answers, proving that his mind is full of basic geometrical concepts, which must be innate (born within his mind).

Plato had no interest in the extreme scepticism we saw in the proof of Gorgias and was particularly scathing about the relativism expressed by Protagoras, in his remark that 'Man is the measure of all things' (see p.31). Plato's response was that if all viewpoints are equally valid, then presumably we should respect the point of view of a tadpole. Also, the truth is what we would expect the gods to agree on, and their judgements are superior to ours. Most tellingly, if you are a relativist you must rate the beliefs of people who disagree with you just as highly as your own beliefs, including your belief in relativism. This is a classic case of turning the tables, showing that a proposed theory doesn't live up to its own principles. Like many of Plato's dialogues, *Theaetetus* ends in a state of uncertainty, but it is the founding text of epistemology.

Plato's metaethics (the general grounds for principles of ethical values) grows out of his theory of Forms. Some Forms are of ordinary things such as horses, but others are of much greater importance, because they govern the whole of reality. Beauty has special significance (as shown in the dialogue *Symposium*), but mainly because it is one of our finest experiences, and leads us on to even higher things. Truth is a second Form to which an especially high value is assigned, but the one supreme Form, which gives purpose to all of the others, is the Form of the Good. Although it is a pure idea, it has a semi-divine status for Plato (and hence a great influence on later religious thought). The Form of the Good not only embodies the nature of moral goodness, but also motivates it, by making what is good the supreme purpose of existence. This preserves and strengthens the traditional Greek view that nature and the cosmos are intrinsically good.

Plato's defence of his metaethics is much more down to earth. In his dialogues such as *Republic* and *Gorgias*, there are characters who are quite cynical, claiming that morality is either rules the strong impose on the weak, or else the rules of justice which the weak pathetically try to impose on the strong. The most dramatic suggestion is in his story of the Ring of Gyges, a ring of invisibility which enabled an ordinary citizen to become a king. How would we all behave if we had such a ring? Moral ideals would soon vanish, it is suggested, because we could get away with any crime, and morality is actually mere fear of being caught.

On the way to answering these claims, Plato explored the philosophy of politics and of mind. In *Republic* he designs an ideal state which contains three main groups: the community of business entrepreneurs, the army, and the wise rulers (the Guardians), who must be philosophers, because wisdom requires an understanding of the Forms. Unusually for the time, Plato allows that talented women could qualify as Guardians. He then describes the mind as a familiar combination of reason and desires, but moderated by an intermediate 'spirit' which acts as the motivator, and can be channelled for or against reason. The three-part model of the mind matches his three-part model of society, and moral goodness is then defined as harmony and order among the three components (which in practice means control by the Guardians and by reason). Hence Plato is in the tradition of Pythagoras, and sees

order as the supreme value of nature, and one to which we should conform. His politics are therefore undemocratic and authoritarian, and his morality is based on reason. A notorious example of his authoritarian approach is the decision to ban arts such as tragedy from his ideal state, on the grounds that they merely imitate reality, thus taking us further away from wisdom instead of promoting it.

When it comes to his normative ethics (deciding the guidelines for an actual good life), he defends the

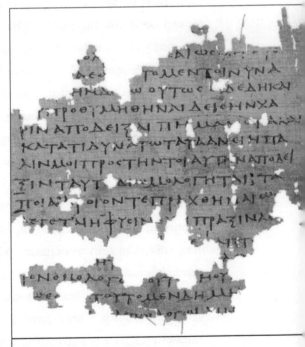

Above: Plato's *Republic* is the earliest great work to survive, covering metaphysics, knowledge, morality, art and politics.

rational practice of virtues of character, and his main focus is on refuting the rival claim that pleasure is good for mankind, a view which he treats with contempt. His simplest argument is that we all know there are bad pleasures, so pleasure can't always be good. He assumes that anyone would rather lose their capacity for pleasure than lose their reason, so reason must be superior. The life of mere pleasure strikes him as no better than the life of a jellyfish, or a life continually scratching itches. And should the gods reward a good life with eternal drunkenness? Plato clearly had a flair for good examples.

In his philosophy of religion, Plato certainly believed in divine powers, and saw the gods as the embodiment of goodness and rationality (despite the weaknesses of character they display in the poems of Homer). Echoing the views of Anaxagoras, he argued that nature must be full of powerful minds, because that is the only possible explanation of movement (since, in our experience, anything which moves itself, rather than being moved, involves a mind). He thus endorsed the traditional slogan that 'all things are full of gods'.

The relation between the gods and moral goodness raised an important question, found in his dialogue *Euthyphro*. Are the gods very wise, and thus understand what is good, or do they create goodness, so that goodness is simply what the gods desire? This Euthyphro Question asks 'Which comes first?', and often crops up in philosophy. Plato's answer is that the Form of the Good comes first, and it is understood and revered by the gods. Evil was explained by Plato (as also by Empedocles) as a more obscure force which was ignorant of the Good.

ARISTOTLE (384–322 BCE)

The genius of Aristotle remains astounding even today. In addition to his philosophy, he also founded the science of biology, single-handedly created formal logic, and was the first literary critic. The son of a doctor in Macedonia in northern Greece, he was sent at the age of 18 to Athens to study in Plato's Academy, where he remained as a pupil for 20 years. After Plato's death he left Athens, and was invited to tutor the heir to the throne of Macedon – a youth we now know as Alexander the Great. He returned to Athens and founded his own school, the Lyceum, where most of his works were written in a clear but very compressed style. Aristotle was forced into exile after the death of Alexander, and died the following year.

Aristotle held that philosophy is motivated by the desire to understand, and began with a sense of both wonder and confusion. He normally started each enquiry by reporting the consensus of common sense, and then wrote a survey of previous books on the topic.

Above: Aristotle was Plato's brilliant pupil, founding his own school, and producing major theories in almost every area of philosophy.

He systematically collected books (possibly creating the first-ever library), and his house in Athens was known as 'the house of the reader'. His aim was always clarity and precision, although he remarked that precision is impossible in some subjects.

Aristotle studied all of the proposals for the first principles of nature, such as water, mathematics, atoms and ideal Forms. He was particularly critical of Plato's theory of Forms, which he felt was obscure and incoherent, explaining nothing. Aristotle preferred the four elements theory, which seemed a good account of what we experience. He rejected the atoms of Democritus because he could not see what would stop endless division, and he rejected the unmoving One of Parmenides, which failed to explain movement, change and diversity. Aristotle is famous for his teleological view of nature – that is, each thing is to be understood in terms of its *telos*, its purpose. We ask of each thing 'what is it for?' or 'what is its function?', and everything natural has a function and purpose. This view is usually rejected by modern science, but we still view human affairs teleologically (asking about the aim of an action), and it throws light on biology (asking what an ear is for).

Aristotle's first step in metaphysics (which he called 'the thinking of thinking') has major importance in the history of philosophy. He pondered the nature of pure Being that was explored by Parmenides and Plato, and concluded that little of any use can be said on the matter, so he turned to the study of particular things. What is an object? When is it unified? To what extent can an object change? How should we categorize objects? Can objects be defined?

Two particular aspects of objects needed explanation. First, how can an object remain the same object even when it changes, and when does change finally destroy the object? Second, what unites the predicates (or features) of an object? If something is red and round and soft, what unifies the three predicates? Aristotle offered a single answer to both of these questions – that there must be some core aspect of an object which both retains its identity through change, and is the basic thing to which the features attach. Some features may be unimportant, but others are essential to its existence, so we must identify 'what-it-is-to-be' that thing. This is Aristotle's well-known Essentialism. In what seem to be his earlier writings he identified the essence of a thing with the answer to the question 'what is it?', which might get the reply 'it's a tomato', but later he saw the essence in the 'form' of the thing, which seems to be its guiding ideas, principles, mechanisms and causal powers.

The target of Aristotle's theory (later known as 'hylo-morphism') is a full definition of a thing, which spells out its essential nature. He outlined procedures for achieving a

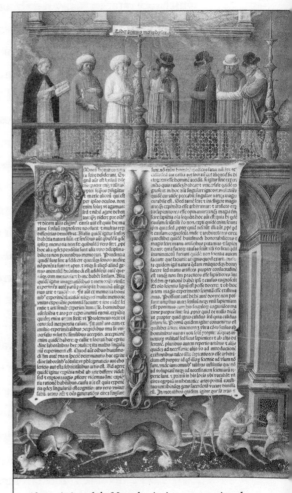

Above: Aristotle's *Metaphysics* is an exceptional work, which concerns our most basic beliefs and concepts about nature and reality.

good definition by specifying the general type and then narrowing down to get as close as possible to this particular thing. Definitions are expressed in language, so they always have to be general because they use universals – single words like 'red' or 'horse' which can refer to many red things or horses.

The questions we ask about objects lead him to a set of categories. So if we ask 'When was it?' we need a category of time, and if we ask 'How big is it?' we need a category of quantity. He arrives at ten categories, which can be used in any explanation or definition. We want to know the thing's essential nature, its quantity, its qualities, its relations, its location, its position, its time, its state, its active powers and its passive powers.

The word 'powers' refers to Aristotle's distinction between potentiality and actuality. Because the explanation of movement was so important for him, and merely cataloguing a thing's visible features won't explain that, he sees active and passive potentialities or powers as a vital component in explanation. Nature continually moves from what is potential at one moment to what is actual at another, so that Becoming and Being are united in a single account of reality. Many potentialities are, of course, never realized, and this was how he viewed infinity – processes which can potentially continue forever, but never reach an actualized destination. Aristotle believed in a remote divine power, because there must be some ultimate source for causation and movement in the cosmos.

Aristotle invented formal logic. It seems that he became interested in the patterns of the arguments used in the Academy, rather than in their content. If someone argues 'If all fruit is nice, and apples are fruit, then apples are nice', we must accept it even if we have never seen an apple. Any argument of the form 'If all x are F, and y is an x, then y must also be F' has to be accepted, no matter what x, y and F refer to. Importantly, we must also accept 'If all fruit is poisonous, and apples are fruit, then apples are poisonous', even though the conclusion is false. Aristotle distinguished between the validity of the argument and the truth of its components, and he devised a way to represent arguments by symbols, to show their structure rather than their content. The examples about apples are 'syllogisms', which offer a pair of statements, and a conclusion to be drawn from them. The two examples given are valid syllogisms, but 'If all apples are fruit, and some fruits are poisonous, then apples must be poisonous' is invalid. Aristotle's logic was the standard system for formalizing arguments for the next two thousand years.

Aristotle's epistemology focused on explanations that bring understanding, rather than Plato's focus on justifications that bring knowledge. He was aware of the problems concerning justification, such as the regress problem – that whatever does the justifying must itself be justified, which could go on forever. But Aristotle laughed at sceptics, who seemed to think that if you push one of your eyes sideways you have created two realities, or that dreams are believable. He was no more sympathetic than Plato to the doubts of relativists about whether any truth is possible. It struck him as absurd that there is nothing more to truth than whether people agree on something, and it seemed obvious that if two people disagree then at least one of them must be wrong (the Principle of Non-Contradiction).

The main aim of an explanation is to give the causes of something, and he offers the example that if you can state the causes of a lunar eclipse then no further explanation is needed. He distinguished four types of explanation, which are mainly four ways in which something can be caused. His example was a statue, and its Material Cause is what the statue is made of. Its Efficient Cause (which is the one modern science focuses on) says what produced the statue, which is the sculptor. The Formal Cause is the statue's essential nature, which concerns its shape and structure, and its Final (or Teleological) Cause is its purpose, perhaps for a temple. A successful explanation will give all four types of cause, and genuine understanding combines these explanations with definitions of the key concepts involved.

Nowadays Aristotle is best known for his thorough account of what we now call Virtue Theory, which presents morality in terms of qualities of character. He started from the idea of Socrates that the main aim is *eudaimonia* (a flourishing life), and agreed with Plato that this consists of harmony within the soul, but he developed that account in greater detail. The soul (*psuchē*) has three parts to it – the rational, the irrational and the vegetative. The vegetative *psuchē* is found in plants as well as in the human body, and is best seen as vitality, with health as its state of virtue or excellence.

Aristotle disagreed with Socrates about *akrasia* (lack of control, or weakness of will), because he thought that reason sometimes fails to control the irrational part of the *psuchē* (so someone might smoke a cigarette, even though their reason says they shouldn't). In humans there are five levels of moral control: a few people are so bad that they are bestial, with no understanding of right and wrong; next come people who do wrong because they misjudge what is right; then come people who do wrong despite knowing what is right (which is *akrasia*); they might then rise to the next level, which is acting well by controlling bad desires; but the highest level (of mental health and true virtue) is eliminating bad desires, so that good deeds come naturally from a harmonious soul, which is controlled by reason. The criterion for deciding when someone has control is whether they are obviously responsible for what they did, so Aristotle proposed some tests for that. (Despite the determinism implied by the atomist views of Democritus, there was no concept of free will at this time).

Aristotle's concept of a virtue is connected to his teleology, which implies that each thing has its own essential function. The good for each thing is to function successfully, just as a knife is good if it cuts well, and a thing is beautiful if it functions perfectly. The essential nature of people is to be social and rational animals. Hence the good for man is to be a healthy animal, to function well as a good citizen, and to reason well.

A social virtue is a habit which leads to the typical behaviour of a good citizen, so the main issue is how this should be achieved. Aristotle rejected the intellectualist view of Socrates (that only knowledge is required), so it is also important to direct the irrational part of the soul, which means we should feel appropriate emotions in each situation. Such responses are habitual, so the emotions of children must be suitably trained. Virtuous behaviour obviously needs intelligence, but (unlike Plato) he doesn't believe that theoretical or philosophical knowledge will do the job. What is needed is *phronesis*, usually translated as 'practical reason', and best understood as common sense.

Each human activity has its own virtue, but all Greeks knew the four cardinal virtues, which are wisdom, courage, self-discipline and moral justice. Aristotle added a few others, such as friendship (but only between virtuous people), and he was unusual in saying that external goods (such as wealth and long life) are also needed for human flourishing. Each virtue is seen as ranging between two extremes, which in the case of courage are foolhardiness and cowardice. The ideal for each virtue is to find its 'mean', which is not a mere average, but what is appropriate for the situation. There are, for example, occasions when a good person should definitely show anger, even though it is usually a bad thing. Aristotle took pleasure (despised by Plato) to be a good thing, provided it remains subordinate and appropriate, because every human activity is improved if we enjoy it.

Aristotle's views on politics were directly implied by this theory of ethics. Man is a social animal, so a society is not a market or an agreement, but a natural state of affairs. The purpose of a society is to allow its citizens to flourish, and the performance of noble deeds is the hallmark of the best societies. His idea of a citizen was very limited by modern standards, since he excluded women, and considered the essential nature of many people to be best suited to slavery. But for those who do qualify, education and the promotion of friendship are chief social aims, and consequently he (again unlike Plato) was a democrat, because friendship needs equality, and education and flourishing need freedom.

CHAPTER 3

SCHOOLS OF PHILOSOPHY (370 BCE-200 CE)

Plato founded a school (the Academy) in Athens, and his pupil Aristotle founded the Lyceum, his own school, just down the road. The main purpose of a philosophical school was to preserve the teachings of its founder, so pupils had to decide which philosopher to study, and only very creative philosophers could found a school. Modern philosophy is mainly studied through books, and students spend their time reading and writing in libraries. In the ancient schools the precious books were read aloud, but the main activity was continuous conversation. This built up great excitement about arguments, which were given names, such as the Master Argument or the Mowing Argument.

Many cities were known for their small schools with distinctive opinions, but the main schools of ancient philosophy were the Platonists, the Peripatetics (who followed Aristotle), the Cynics, the Cyrenaics, the Epicureans, the Stoics, the Sceptics, the Eclectics, the Pythagoreans, and the Neo-Platonists. Some of these schools had a home base, but others were just grouped together by their doctrines. In the early part of this period Athens was the headquarters of philosophy, and was dominated by four schools: the Academy of Plato, the Lyceum of Aristotle, the Garden of Epicurus, and the Stoa of Zeno of Citium. Athens gradually waned in influence, and its schools were closed after the ruthless looting of the city by the Roman general Sulla in 87 BCE. Subsequently the main centre for Greek philosophy was Alexandria, on the African coast. The ancient schools were effectively ended in 529 CE by the Emperor Justinian.

CYRENAICS AND CYNICS

The main aim of Socrates was to defend the life of virtue, and therefore to attack a life devoted to pleasure. Plato agreed with him, though Aristotle included pleasure among the goods of a virtuous life. In the city of Cyrene, in north Africa, Aristippus and

Above: The ruins of Cyrene, where pure pleasure was thought to be the greatest good for mankind.

his grandson (also Aristippus) took the opposite approach, and wholeheartedly endorsed pleasure as the sole good for mankind. They were struck by the isolation of each human being, and so they did not value friendship, and could see nothing more to reality than private experiences, which were dominated by pleasures (both intellectual and physical). Since a life of virtue seemed to be mere fashion, the Cyrenaics were very tolerant of people's vices, and simply aimed to re-educate them. They were unusual in denying that life has a single purpose (*telos*), and they championed social freedom as the best means to achieve pleasure.

The Cyrenaics were quite isolated, but the Cynics became famous (or notorious) throughout the Greek world. Many thinkers were as much inspired by the life of Socrates as by his thought, and the Cynics copied his simplicity, his relative poverty and his steely powers of self-control (as when he walked barefoot on ice while on a military campaign). The first Cynic, Antisthenes, had known Socrates personally and aimed to emulate his life. He disliked pleasure so much that he said he would rather go mad than experience it, and seems to have been the first thinker to propose Pantheism – that nature is the only divinity. A later Cynic, Crates of Thebes, gave away his considerable wealth in order to live the Cynic life, and he and his wife Hipparchia (herself a respected philosopher) were a famous couple, living on the streets of Athens.

The best-documented Cynic is Diogenes of Sinope (403–324 BCE). Today he might be described as a hippy or an anarchist, but he was a serious philosopher. 'Cynic' means 'dog-like', and he was happy to live like a dog. He usually slept in a large wine jar in the Athens marketplace and scandalized fellow citizens by masturbating in public, with the remark that he wished hunger was as easily solved. He was very blunt in argument: when someone argued that motion is impossible, he got up and walked away, and when the Platonists defined man as a 'featherless biped', he released a plucked chicken into the Academy.

His life was inimitable, but many of his teachings were very influential. He extended the idea that nature was divine, and urged that the good life for man must conform to what is natural. It is notable that where most of the schools were aimed at a specialist elite, Diogenes' teachings (like those of Socrates) were available for everyone. He taught that indifference was a virtue, so as to avoid the pains of a complex social life. Most unusually for his time, he was not loyal to one city, but called himself a 'citizen of the world', and he considered free speech to be the greatest civic virtue. Because he lived a long and public life he achieved great fame, but none of his ten books have survived.

Above: The belief of Diogenes in the simplest possible existence was lived out in public, and made him a famous but controversial figure.

THE EPICUREANS

Epicurus (341–270 BCE) was born on the island of Samos and founded a school in Athens, close to the Academy, in 306 BCE. Called The Garden, his school seems to have been a delightful place, devoted to peaceful pleasure, friendship and conversation. A few of Epicurus' writings survive, but our best account of his views is in *On the Nature of the Universe* by the Roman poet and philosopher

Lucretius, written in around 70 BCE. The two biggest influences on the thinking of Epicurus were the ideas of Democritus and the rejection of the ideas of Plato. The latter believed in a higher reality of pure ideals, understood through dialectical conversations, but Epicurus laughed at that and was only interested in the physical world, which he took to be made entirely of atoms. His main argument was that matter cannot be infinitely divisible, so division must eventually meet objects which cannot be divided. He agreed with Democritus that there are innumerable shapes and sizes of atoms which spontaneously move within a void and link together to form groups which are the visible objects. Democritus said atoms were basically just a shape and a size, but Epicurus said their weight was also basic. The familiar qualities of objects, such as hardness and colour, arise from combinations of the three basic features.

Above: Epicurus rejected high ideals, and said reality is entirely physical, and cautious pleasure is its greatest good.

Epicurus believed in the existence of the gods (because the idea of gods is imprinted in our minds), but held that they were made of atoms, and very detached from our world. In response to the idea that lightning is hurled by the gods, he asked why it is never hurled from a blue sky. He said the gods don't answer prayers, because prayers are often for the destruction of enemies, which would be catastrophic. Hence the cosmos is self-sufficient, and Epicurus endorsed the unusual Cyrenaic view that nature has no purpose. He argued that the cosmos is eternal, but if it did have a beginning it couldn't have been designed by the gods, because it contains too many imperfections.

If everything is made entirely of atoms, then that includes us, and it has considerable implications; our understanding of the world comes from our atoms interacting with other atoms. Epicurus was an empiricist, who not only relied on sense experience, but considered it virtually infallible (at least for each individual person). Delusions and dreams do not undermine the senses, because they are just true facts about our minds. Reason is not separate, but arises from our senses, and only the senses can reveal truth. The mind itself (the *psuchē*, or soul) is also physical, consisting of the movement of many very smooth atoms. To those who say that *psuchē* must be a foundation of nature, Epicurus says there is nothing unusual about remarkable things emerging from simple beginnings, as when a chicken emerges from an egg. If human beings can laugh, that doesn't mean we are made of humorous atoms.

An important consequence of the mind being the mere movement of physical atoms is that the atoms then seem to control everything, and it is only a delusion that human beings make free choices. This is the first appearance of the important idea that determinism is true (that the future is wholly inevitable), and so there is no 'freedom of the will'. Epicurus spotted the worry that if we cannot make choices, we cannot be held responsible for our good or evil deeds, which seemed to defy common sense. He therefore added a surprising idea to the atomism of Democritus – that instead of the atoms moving in inevitable straight lines, there is an occasional 'swerve' in the movement which cannot be explained. Since such swerves occur in our *psuchē*, our decisions have an element of freedom. Few thinkers believe that Epicurus thereby solved the problem of free will (since we don't seem able to control the swerves), but this was the beginning of a debate which has run for centuries.

When a person dies their atoms are dispersed, and their capacity to experience things depends on their atoms. Hence for human beings there can be no afterlife. Facing this fact may make us very fearful of death, but Epicurus argued that this is absurd. We shouldn't fear an event which is remote from us before our last day, and when we do die we are no longer there to experience it. Being dead is not frightening, because it is identical to the situation before we were born, and no one fears that. However, Epicureans say that suicide is rarely justifiable, even when faced with a disaster such as going blind. Disgrace is not a good reason to kill oneself, pain and misery can be endured, and there is nearly always hope of regaining the pleasures of life.

Because experience is the basis of our existence, the good for humans is pleasure. This again shows the influence of the Cyrenaics, but Epicurus is very restrained on the subject. We must plan ahead, so constant drunkenness may be fun, but it produces hangovers and ruins your health. The supreme good is friendship, which is a continual and harmless delight. The highest priority is the avoidance of pain, and especially mental pain, which persists for much longer. In reply to the claims of Socrates and Plato that virtue is superior to pleasure, he argued that the two are almost the same, because the life of restrained pleasure is virtuous, and being virtuous is one of the highest pleasures. Justice, he said, is not a pure ideal, but simply a matter of keeping contracts and agreements (as we would expect among good friends).

THE STOICS

Zeno of Citium came to Athens from Cyprus and studied with Crates the Cynic until the shameless Cynic lifestyle became too much for him. He studied at other schools, including the

Above: The ruins of the Painted Stoa, where Zeno founded his Stoic school. Their very influential writings are now mostly lost.

Academy, before founding his own school in a public arcade called the Painted Stoa, giving us the word 'stoic'. The Stoic school endured for several centuries. In its early stages stoic theories were thorough and complex, and the great thinkers were Zeno, Cleanthes and Chrysippus, but none of their books survive. In the later Roman period a more popular stoic lifestyle was presented in surviving writings by Seneca, Epictetus and Marcus Aurelius. The doctrines are consistent across both periods, so we can give a general description.

By 301 BCE, when the Stoic school was founded, many philosophy books had been written and strong traditions established. The new school adopted some teachings and reacted against others. The most important starting point was admiration of the cynic idea that we should live according to nature, but as human nature is rational, it is absurd to live like a dog. The Stoics designed a curriculum for their new school and divided philosophy into three major topics – reason, character and nature – each with numerous subdivisions.

The Stoics saw in the new syllogistic logic of Aristotle a tool for improving arguments. They extended logic to cover complete sentences, and spotted a number of basic logical truths, of which the simplest became known as Modus Ponens: if one proposition implies another proposition, and the first proposition is true, then the second one must be true too. That is, implication transmits truth, which is the basis of all reasoning. Unlike the Epicureans, they admired Plato's ideal of dialectical reasoning, even though they said that Plato's Forms were merely human thoughts.

Placing a supreme value on logic and dialectic, the Stoics also adopted the idea that nature itself is rational. Their two main arguments for this were that the cosmos is perfect, and hence it must obviously embody perfect rationality, and also that the cosmos produces rational beings, which would be impossible if nature were not rational. Zeno compared this to an olive tree that produced well-tuned flutes, which would prove that harmony was in the tree.

The epicurean account of knowledge (based on the infallibility of sense experiences) was also rejected by the Stoics. They agreed that experience is crucial, but described three steps to knowledge. Perception is the first step, but the vital second step was to 'grasp' the perception, by giving it full attention. Even then it only fully qualified as known if reason could see no possibility of the perception being false. Zeno compared the three stages to holding something in your palm, then closing your fist around it, then holding your fist with your other hand.

When it came to character and ethics, they faced the new problem of determinism and free will, but rejected the epicurean swerve of the atoms, because it contradicts the rationality of nature. Stoics generally accepted determinism, although Chrysippus tried to find a compromise position. A famous image is that we are like a dog tied to a moving cart by a string – we can choose to follow the cart, but if we don't then we must follow it anyway. On the *akrasia* problem (of why we knowingly do things that harm us) they sided with Socrates against Aristotle, saying that such apparent stupidity is actually rational. This is not because reason rules the emotional mind, but because the tempting desires themselves are rational, and yearnings for money or drink are judgements that such things are good.

The joint sources of stoic values were reason and nature. The hallmark of rational values was agreement, and so the highest values were those containing no conflicts. The secondary values were the natural ones, arising from the requirements of ordinary life. The Stoics rejected Aristotle's belief in external goods such as money and honour, asserting that only a virtuous character can produce a good life. Virtue was an all-or-nothing achievement: either you were a fully virtuous person, or you were a failure. Goodness was equated with beauty, making a good life a work of art. We rightly associate stoicism with determined endurance of suffering, but the Stoics also (unlike the Epicureans) saw suicide as legitimate. Seneca committed suicide when his political position was hopeless, but wrote that it might sometimes be our duty to battle on for the sake of family.

An important principle that emerges from stoic ideas is that justice is not just human convention but a self-evident fact of nature. When states create laws they shouldn't just make up what is convenient, because reason and nature reveal the objective truth about justice. This begins the tradition of Natural Law, which had a huge influence on later legal thinking. In agreement with Diogenes, the Stoics also saw themselves as citizens of the whole world, and so natural justice is also universal justice.

The Stoics' view of nature was teleological (purposeful). They again rejected Epicurus, because the rationality of nature implied both an ultimate purpose and a supreme divinity. Realizing that natural evils such as earthquakes were a difficulty for this view, they asserted that the cosmos was entirely good if you could see the whole picture. They agreed with Aristotle that there are four elements, and also that there are basic categories of existence, which are substrate, quality, disposition and relation. Hence reality can be understood entirely as objects with properties and powers, organized according to relationships. The human mind is no exception to this, because it is a part of the natural world. Cleanthes argued that wounds causing pain and shameful thoughts causing blushing show how intimately mind and body are united. This seems to make survival of death impossible, but they saw the *psuchē* as a refined form of air and fire, which could remain in existence if the person was virtuous.

THE SCEPTICS

The great schools of the Epicureans and the Stoics built on the doctrines of the Platonists, Aristotelians and Cynics by accepting some views and challenging others. In the background, though, more radical thinking was at work, inspired by the grave doubts about truth and knowledge expressed by the early Sophists. Pyrrho of Elis lived at the same time as Epicurus and Zeno of Citium, and turned the old sceptical arguments into a way of life. He was struck by the idea that every argument was cancelled out by an equal and opposite argument, and concluded that a wise person should embrace the resulting intellectual paralysis. He accepted the aim of Diogenes in philosophy, which was peace of mind achieved by indifference. Pyrrho's strategy was to suspend judgement on everything, unless it was totally obvious. He introduced the idea that the big problem for philosophers was to find 'the criterion' – the decisive test for whether or not a belief was actually true. He wrote nothing, but was a great role model for later Sceptics.

Scepticism came to the fore in Athens in 264 BCE, when Plato's Academy surprisingly adopted many sceptical views, mainly in opposition to the confidence about knowledge expressed by the Stoics. Our main knowledge of the sceptical arguments comes

Above: Pyrrho (who was famously absent-minded)
made scepticism into a way of life, and taught
detachment from beliefs and commitments.

from some fascinating surviving books by Sextus Empiricus of around 200 CE. Most of these arguments aim to show that finding the criterion for knowledge is impossible, and they attack all the schools which have clear positive doctrines because they are uncritical and 'dogmatic'.

The two basic sceptical arguments were that all reasoning cancels out, and that definitions are impossible. Their other arguments attack all possible criteria, and especially those which rely on perception. If I offer some fact (such as a rational insight, or an experience) as a justification for a belief, there is an obvious problem. I have to be sure of the supporting fact – but that needs a further justification. The Sceptics said this can only go one of three ways: the string of justifications ends in a fact which needs no justification; the justifications go round in a circle and support one another; or the string of justifications goes on forever. This 'trilemma' means that justification is impossible, they said. We have assumed that all knowledge needs justification. If the justifications go round in a circle they could all be wrong (like mutually supporting lies). And if they go on forever then we never reach anything which is securely known.

The attacks on perception were summarized in the Ten Modes of scepticism (which also support relativism – the view that truth entirely depends on viewpoint). They draw attention to factors which can distort a perception, such as our prior expectations, possible disease of the sense organs, unusual conditions, and misleading comparisons. Perceptions also depend on who is doing the viewing, which is affected by the species of animal, the local culture, the particular individual doing the sensing, and which sense is involved. Confronting all of those problems should destroy anyone's faith in sense perception. An obvious reply to extreme scepticism is to turn the tables, and accuse the Sceptics of *knowing* that scepticism is true, which would be absurd. The standard sceptical reply is to concede the point, and agree that they don't even know their own theory. Extreme scepticism was quietly forgotten for many centuries, but once it resurfaced it became a permanent challenge which all philosophers must face up to.

THE NEO-PLATONISTS

After Aristotle decided that questions about the essential nature of Being should just focus on objects and their properties the very general questions about metaphysics were neglected, but Plotinus (204–270 CE) turned once again to the big ideas of Pythagoras, Parmenides and Plato. He had studied in Alexandria and then moved to Rome, where he became a famous teacher who included women among his pupils and wrote his great book *The Enneads*. His interest in lofty ideals was probably a rebellion against the excessive materialism of the Stoics. His main interest was in the claim of Parmenides that ultimate Being is the eternal and unchanging One (concealed by the shifting appearances of our world), and Plato's idea that the Form of the Good is the source of reality.

Plotinus accepted Aristotle's criticism of The One of Parmenides – that because it is eternal and unchanging, it offers no explanation of movement and change in the visible world. The problem was that the One is taken to be the essence of Being, and so should contain all the principles of existence, including movement. Hence the ultimate explanation must be prior to and beyond Being, and

Above: Plotinus was the most idealistic of philosophers, turning Plato's theory of reality into lofty spiritual vision.

the Form of the Good, being a pure ideal, could play that role. So the key idea of Plotinus was to adopt the idea of The One, but to see it as beyond Being, in the perfect realm of platonic Forms.

From this initial idea of The One which transcends Being, he then built a three-part system for the essential structure of nature. Being is a necessary consequence of the perfection of The One, and radiates from it as light does from the Sun. Being is rational, and so the second phase of existence is *Nous*, which might translate as 'Intellectual-Principle', and is the realm of the gods. This rational mode of Being produces an utterance (*logos*), which gives rise in its turn to the third phase of nature, which is Soul (*Psuchē*). The influence of Pythagoras is seen in a further stage, that Soul produces numbers, which are the source of individual objects, and Soul is also the source of life.

Soul is the mind of human beings, and Plotinus argues for the perfect unity of the mind, and for dualism (that mind is quite separate from the body). In the body, he argues, the arm is quite unaware of the leg, but in the mind all parts are wholly aware of other parts, so mind is quite different from body. Also matter is seen as an inferior mode of Being, and the mind must be quite different, to be elevated above it. There is less emphasis than in Plato on the moral aspect of this picture, but the concepts of right and good are an intrinsic part of the Intellectual-Principle, and so Plotinus offers us an account of morality that is based on pure reason.

The Neo-Platonist tradition was maintained by Porphyry (234–305), a pupil of Plotinus, who edited his teacher's long and complex book. One of Porphyry's pupils was Iamblichus (245–325), who not only maintained the doctrines of Plotinus, but also wrote a biography of Pythagoras, and emphasized the role of numbers in the new system. Pythagorean doctrines, and their disciplined way of life, had revived in the first century CE, and the movement had become increasingly religious, but around this time the Pythagoreans seem to have merged with the Neo-Platonists.

Not all philosophers of this time belonged to a specific school, and a group of philosophers in the first century BCE are referred to as the Eclectics, meaning that they chose for themselves the best bits from several different schools. The most interesting of these is Cicero (106–43 BCE), who was a great Roman statesman and orator. In his youth he had studied in the Greek schools of Rhodes, and wrote several works of philosophy, most of which survive. He was not an original thinker, but he records arguments in dialogue form with great clarity, and picks his way among the theories very perceptively.

The schools of philosophy were mostly Greek, in their traditions and language, and so their decline was hastened by the decline of

Greek culture and the conquest of Greek cities. When the Roman Empire turned to Christianity it gradually became less tolerant of pagan religions and free critical thought, and so the ancient schools were diluted in their teaching, and then faded away.

CHAPTER 4

PHILOSOPHY FOR CHRISTIANITY (380–1347)

At first the decline of Greek culture and the dominance of Christianity in the Roman Empire were a disaster for philosophers. Gradually, though, it was realized that the surviving Greek texts raised challenging questions for Christian theologians, even though some of these old ideas were unacceptable, or even shocking. Christianity struggled for survival once the Roman Empire collapsed, but it gradually regained its leading position in European thought, supported by priests and monks, and by the foundation of universities. There followed a lively period in which religious faith confronted the most challenging questions asked by philosophers. The resulting conflict between free reasoning and church authority was inevitable, but not before some major works of philosophy had been created.

AUGUSTINE OF HIPPO (354–430)

Early in the fourth century CE the Emperor of Rome converted to Christianity. As the authority of Christianity increased, the schools of Greek philosophy came under pressure and were eventually closed down. Their writings might have been entirely destroyed in the years that followed were it not for the work in North Africa of Augustine, Bishop of Hippo, who learned about Greek thought through Cicero, and was familiar with the ideas of the Neo-Platonists. He thus started a tradition in theology of treating the best pagan thinking with great respect.

At first Augustine's religion was unorthodox, but he then became the leading critic of 'heresy'. He rejected the Manicheans, whose materialistic theory saw the light of the human soul as trapped in the dark of the body, and also the Pelagians, who thought we could escape from the original sin which began the human race. For Augustine, being trapped in a body *is* original sin, but we must struggle to ascend into a more spiritual realm.

The ascent from materialism requires reason and language. Language must connect to the world, but it can also rise above it. Our mind unites our experiences, but reason sees what is necessarily true, and also unites us to other souls, from which the body separates us. Augustine was always struck by human limitations, however, and said that such knowledge is a gift of God, in moments of 'illumination', rather than our own achievement. Hence we must be willing to accept authority about knowledge, and to believe things before we understand them.

Whether Fate controls our lives was treated by Augustine as a question about the human will, and its ability to free itself from outside influences when it makes choices. He defended the idea that we are free to choose our future, even though God knows exactly what we will choose. What concerned him most was how people can control the evil in their own lives, because the

Above: After an unorthodox start, Augustine developed the
philosophical theories needed to underpin Christianity.

salvation of the soul is at stake. Since the soul is not trapped in
the body, it is free to improve and escape the evils of materialism,
and this can be achieved by the rational will. However, the
presence of original sin is irrational and a huge burden, and it
prevents the will from being wholly rational. Augustine became
increasingly pessimistic about this, and felt that our only hope
is through the grace of God, which meant that salvation is a
gift, and most people face eternal damnation. He nevertheless
thought that happiness in this life is possible, and his attitude to
morality is summarized in the memorable slogan 'Love, and do
what you will.'

Augustine wrote a particularly interesting discussion of time. If God is an eternal being existing beyond the physical world, then how does this relate to daily life? Can a timeless being intervene in events? Does an eternal being exist at all times, or outside of time? A tree can exist, but how can a year exist, since neither the past nor the future seem to exist? But if periods of time don't exist, how can an event be due to happen 'in ten days' time'? As he memorably put it, he understood time perfectly, as long as he didn't think about it! He could not decide whether time might just be physical movement, or not real at all, or merely a feature of our minds.

Before Augustine, history was often seen as moving in repeating cycles, but he spelled out the Christian idea that there is a direction in history, moving from the Old Testament to the New Testament, and then to a day of judgement. This shaped much later debates about whether history contains inevitable processes and purposes. He also raised the important topic in political philosophy of whether it is ever morally right to declare war.

BOETHIUS (c.477–524)

As the Roman Empire declined, the scholar and logician Boethius became caught up in worldly affairs and spent the rest of his life in prison, awaiting execution. In response he wrote his *Consolations of Philosophy*, which was widely read. Although he was a Christian, he found his main consolation in Neo-Platonist philosophy.

The two most influential topics addressed by Boethius were whether we have free will and the nature of universals. He accepted that Fate controls worldly and physical things, but said that reason can reveal to us a divine reality where the necessity no longer applies. We must have free will, he claimed, simply because we are rational (an influential opinion). He also saw the difficulty for free choice if God has foreknowledge of what will happen. His response was that the future is not necessitated just because it is known. We don't assume that the present moment is necessitated, just because we know what is happening, and my knowing what is about to happen doesn't make it the only thing that *could* happen.

Above: Boethius was a lonely hero of philosophy, developing his platonist ideas during a long spell in prison.

Universals are single words or concepts which can refer to many things, such as 'white' or 'tree'. The puzzle is to explain the mode of existence of something which is 'one-over-many'. If you see two red tomatoes you see two objects, but do you see one colour or two instances of the same colour? Realists say there are two tomatoes, but the redness which they share is a real third item. Nominalists say there are only two things visible, and not three; 'red' is just a name for the coloured aspect of each object.

An example of the importance of the problem for theologians is the Christian doctrine of The Trinity, which says that God is three beings – Father, Son and Holy Spirit – which are also one being. The unity of The Trinity must come from all three beings sharing the same attributes. If there are just these three individuals, as

Nominalists say, then unity is impossible. Peter Abelard came close to being stoned to death by a mob for apparently believing in three Gods rather than one. In modern thought universals are vital to the way we classify nature and express its general laws, and for any expression of general truths in language.

Standard theories said universals either exist separately ('before the thing'), or as part of each particular entity ('in the thing'), or just as mental concepts ('following the thing'). Boethius addressed the anti-universals argument which said that anything that exists must be single, but universals are many and therefore can't exist. He replied that the universal is 'abstracted' by the mind (from many white things, or many trees), just as geometers abstract pure lines from the physical world. This is not, however, merely 'following the thing', because the universal is not invented, but precisely follows reality.

ISLAM (900–1200)

After Boethius there followed 500 years during which there was little sign of secular philosophy in Europe. Christian thinking was very conservative, and gradually the manuscripts of ancient Greek texts, mostly held in monasteries, were neglected and destroyed. Apart from the writings of Augustine and Boethius, European philosophy might well have vanished without the contribution of two great Islamic thinkers, both of whom knew the works of Aristotle very well.

Ibn Sina (c.975–1037), known in Europe as Avicenna, lived in what is now Iran. A doctor, he was the leading thinker of the Islamic world. His principle interests in philosophy were the use of logic to achieve a unified system of knowledge, and the nature of the soul and its ways of acquiring understanding. His most famous work is *The Healing*, which concerns the health of the soul.

He took from Aristotle the idea that logic primarily consists of definitions and syllogisms, which apply to scientific method, as well as to pure reasoning. The key to scientific explanation is to guess the 'middle term' of the syllogism which implies some given fact. Thus if the fact is that 'Socrates is mortal', the explanation is given by seeing that Socrates is the member of some category, and that this category has the essential nature of being mortal. Once we see that the middle term is that Socrates 'is a man', we understand the fact. For Avicenna all knowledge follows this model, and he turned the scientific writings of Aristotle into syllogisms in order to show their truth. He considered knowledge to be the essence of human happiness.

Above: Ibn Sina (or Avicenna) produced a great philosophical system within the Muslim tradition.

Like most thinkers of this period, he saw the soul as restrained by the physical world, but always trying to break free into a spiritual world of reason and knowledge. The soul has five internal senses, which aspire to knowledge: common sense, imagery (to store forms of things), imagination, judgement and memory. The soul must be trained to think logically and to see the wider picture, but even this may only bear fruit in the afterlife. In the twelfth century the works of Avicenna were translated into Latin, and he became a major influence on European thought.

Ibn Rushd (1126–1198), known in Europe as Averroes, lived in southern Spain, and was famed for his extensive commentaries on the writings of Aristotle, of whom he was a faithful follower. His careful study of Aristotle's *Physics* had a great influence on attitudes to science and nature. He considered metaphysics to be a quite separate area of study, and thought its importance was overrated by Avicenna. He had to defend his study of philosophy, which he said is the route to virtue, which makes the sciences of nature possible, and thus leads to human happiness. His philosophy is a critical evaluation of Aristotle, rather than a mere account of it, and he helped to create the atmosphere of academic debate which soon flourished in Europe.

ANSELM OF CANTERBURY (1034–1109)

It is a sign of the Latin-speaking culture of Europe at this time that Anselm was born in Italy but ended his life as Archbishop of Canterbury in England. Monasteries were becoming lively centres of learning, and universities were being founded. At the beginning of this great revival, Anselm decided that faith is not enough, and we need to understand religion. His modern fame rests on his quest for an argument for God's existence which did not rely on evidence, and which revealed for us the essential nature of God.

He started from the Old Testament remark that 'the fool hath said in his heart that there is no God', and looked for an argument which even a fool could not deny. At first he argued that the existence and perfections of the world must have an ultimate and supreme source, but that depended on facts about the world, so he then changed his focus to the mere concept that we have of God. We all have the concept of a being 'than which none greater can be conceived', and this must combine all the perfections which we can imagine some 'being' as possessing.

It seems clear that among the perfections of the being must be existence, because for such a being failure to exist would be an imperfection in the concept. Hence this being must

Above: Anselm aimed to clarify Christian belief, and developed a challenging new argument for God's existence.

exist, and that has to be actual existence, and not just imagined existence. Thus if we clearly conceive of God, we see that God necessarily exists. In the course of the argument we have also understood the perfections of God, so we have greatly increased our understanding of what we had believed in by faith alone. This is the Ontological Argument for God's existence, and appeals to believers who feel there just 'has to be' a God, but frustrates non-believers, who struggle to identify where the argument fails. A monk named Guanilo immediately objected that if we try to conceive a perfect island, that too would have to exist for similar reasons, but Anselm said that was a quite different case. The status of the concept of existence has been debated ever since.

The modern fame of Anselm rests on this argument, but he also discussed major issues such as free will. Anselm's concept of truth is not the modern idea of 'getting it right', but is rather the correctness of each thing doing what it ought to do, so that for the will, truth is behaving correctly.

PETER ABELARD (1079–1142)

Even though his written works were not well known, Peter Abelard was very influential because he was a charismatic and controversial teacher who attracted large crowds of students. He thus achieved great fame, which was increased by his well-documented tragic love affair with Heloise. He was the greatest logician of his time, and studied language by carefully cataloguing the role of nouns, verbs, adjectives and adverbs in logical thought. Names, for example, have two aspects to their meaning, so that the name 'Aristotle' both picks out a particular physical being, and also calls to mind the ideas we have about the man.

Abelard argued that real universals are impossible, because their existence leads to contradictions, such as that a human is a type of 'animal', when animals are both rational and irrational, whereas humans are just rational. Such terms for natural kinds (like 'animal' or 'tree') are just things grouped by their similarity, rather than having some special mode of existence. When things are grouped together, the members or parts of the group comes first, and the group doesn't have the properties of the parts (so the concept 'tree' has no leaves). Hence the group is just a label, and not a genuine universal. Universals are merely names, and only objects actually exist, which makes Abelard the first champion of the influential idea of Nominalism.

Abelard rejected many of the standard concepts of metaphysics. He said there are no propositions apart from sentences in a language (which are just constructions from verbal components). Events are not distinct things. No time exists apart from the present moment. Relationships between things do not have their own existence. Whole things just consist of parts, and do not contain a separate 'form' to organize them. He rejected the theory that we think when our mind 'conforms' to the world, because when you think something is 'big' your mind doesn't become big! Thought is just given to us, and cannot be analysed.

Abelard fearlessly discussed morality, when most medieval thinkers avoided the topic, because there was a gulf between Greek ethics and the teaching of the New Testament. He said, for example, that the men who crucified Jesus were just doing their duty, and had done nothing wrong, because what matters is intentions, rather than consequences. He emphasized his view by pointing to cases of moral luck. You are still a charitable person if your charity money is stolen from you, and even incest is no crime if you are ignorant of the facts, because no desire is evil in itself. What is right or good arises from the needs of social life, but moral perfection is only possible in an afterlife.

Abelard wanted religious belief to be rational, and analysed the concept of The Trinity by making careful distinctions between different meanings of 'identity'. However, he always took rationality to be limited (with over-reliance on it leading to heresy), and the obscurities of language made a fully clear faith impossible.

THOMAS AQUINAS (1225–1274)

The Dominican monk Thomas Aquinas came from Italy but travelled widely and was based for a long period in Paris, as well as in Rome and Naples. Like Abelard, he was a master of the public disputation, and his extensive writings, which made him famous, eventually became the basis for the official theology of the Church of Rome.

He was able to read almost the complete works of Aristotle, as well as the commentaries on them by Averroes. Aquinas set out to combine the pagan wisdom of Aristotle with the doctrines of Christianity. He relied on definitions, and on the distinction between what is potential and what is actual, just as Aristotle did, and he wrote in the dialectical style of his public debates, first giving a view, then objections, then replies which give his own view.

He rejected Plato's theory of Forms, on the grounds that if 'human' implies being many things then Socrates is many things, and if it implies being one thing then Socrates and Plato are one thing, which are both absurd. He preferred the hylomorphism of

Aristotle, which sees the form as the essence of each object, and thus explains the thing, largely by specifying what kind of thing it is. The mind can 'abstract' these forms from objects and consider them in isolation, and in this way universals have reality (and so he rejected Nominalism).

Aquinas strongly defended human free will, which he took to be essential for moral responsibility. He saw our rationality as the basis of free will. The will in itself is partly irrational and has little freedom, because it must act according to what is seen as good, and it is reason which decides the nature of that good. Hence Aquinas offered a model for those who want to combine rationality with religious faith.

The clearest statements of the rational arguments for God's existence are found in the writings of Aquinas. He decided that the Ontological Argument of Anselm was invalid, because it required the essential nature of God to be self-evident to human reason. Aquinas observed that what is self-evident in itself may not be self-evident to human beings, and that knowledge of the essence of God is beyond our abilities, so the

Above: Aquinas' careful integration of Aristotelian and Christian teaching soon made him the official theologian of the Chuch of Rome.

argument cannot get started. In its place Aquinas gave his famous Five Ways to prove that God exists.

The First Way says the universe contains movement, and there must be some ultimate power (the First Mover) to get this started. The Second says that each event has a cause, which needs a previous cause, so there must be some First Cause which began the whole sequence. These two ways imply that the universe had a beginning, but whether the universe was created or eternal had long been disputed, so the Third Way proves there is a God even in an eternal universe. We judge that nothing in the universe *has* to exist, which means that the non-existence of each thing is possible. But given infinite time, everything which *could* cease to exist *will* cease to exist, meaning that at some stage nothing existed at all. Since things do now exist, there must be some being with necessary existence (that is, could never fail to exist) which makes this renewal possible.

The Fourth Way is based on the fact that qualities have gradations, such as being hotter or being more true. Each of these aspires to or is understood according to the maximum of that quality, such as what is perfectly true, or the hottest possible. These perfections are only possible if they derive from a supreme perfection, which is God. The Fifth Way is based on Aristotle's teleological view that everything exists for some purpose. Things with no intelligence only gain their purpose from an intelligence (like an arrow directed by an archer), so some supreme intelligence must be the source of all design and purpose.

The core of Aristotle's theory of ethics, based on virtues of character, is the existence of the traditional Four Cardinal Virtues, which are wisdom, courage, self-control and justice.

Aquinas accepted his theory, but added three 'theological' virtues (from the New Testament) which are faith, hope and charity (or love). While the older virtues can be acquired through reason and education, the theological virtues can only be achieved through the grace of God.

In his social thought Aquinas is a great champion of natural law, and of the concept of a just war. He endorsed the idea that law is rooted in nature because Aristotle had shown how we deduce what is good from human nature. Hence Aquinas says that a law created by a tyrant is not a law at all, because it is not based on such reasoning. He argued that there are three conditions which can make a war just: if it is fought for a just cause, or if it is begun on proper authority, or if it is aimed at advancing good or avoiding evil. Modern theorists usually add that a war must have a reasonable chance of success, and be waged with moderation, but this important line of thought was started by Aquinas.

JOHN DUNS SCOTUS (c.1266–1308)

John Duns Scotus (John, from Duns in Scotland) was an academic monk of the Franciscan order, who trained in Oxford then taught at the prestigious University of Paris before being moved to Cologne, where he died.

Thomas Aquinas had accepted most of the teachings of Aristotle, but Duns Scotus took a more critical view. Most importantly, he rejected the main view of existence in Aristotle's hylomorphism, which claimed a distinction between the form or essence of a thing and its actual existence as matter, and thus implied two different modes of existence. For Duns Scotus something either exists or it doesn't (the 'univocal' view), and a form can have no independent existence. Unlike Aristotle and Aquinas, he was also willing to accept the existence of matter which has no form, and of matter which has more than one form (such as a human who is a soul and a body).

Nevertheless, the main type of being is found in distinct substances, so the most important task is to be able to distinguish substances from each other. This is not easy, because we only experience the qualities of a substance, rather than the underlying and hidden 'substrate', and it is unclear when qualities are sufficiently united to be a substance. His discussion of this is so careful that he earned the nickname 'the Subtle Doctor'. He showed that the distinctions we make between things might be in reality, or in possibilities, or merely in our concepts. He proposed the unusual idea that each thing which is distinct has a property unique to that thing (a 'haecceity') which gives it individuality, such as what makes this man Socrates, apart from his many other qualities. Duns Scotus defended (against the Nominalists) the real existence of universals, and the haecceity of each thing 'contracts' the universal into that individual, which thus explains how a universal can be both many things and one thing.

He devised his own long and complex argument for God's existence. It uses many of the ingredients found in Aquinas' Five Ways, such as the need for a first cause, and for a being who embodies the perfections, and he carefully argued that all of these reasons combine to prove the existence of a supreme being, which must be both infinite and unique.

Augustine had proposed the influential idea that humans only have a capacity for knowledge because divine 'illumination' is possible, and this idea still persisted despite criticisms by

Aquinas. Duns Scotus brought the theory to an end by showing that the human intellect has sufficient power to achieve unaided knowledge. He worked through the different kinds of knowledge, such as what we learn from self-evidence, or from experience, or from introspection, and showed how each can be achieved by the natural powers of the intellect. He also disagreed with the claim of Aquinas that human freedom is found in our reason, and defended instead the 'voluntarist' view that the will itself has its own freedom of choice, irrespective of the reasons or the desires which it faces.

WILLIAM OF OCKHAM (c.1287–1347)

William was born in the village of Ockham, southwest of London, and became a Franciscan monk. For a long time he taught at Oxford University, but his commentaries were judged to be unorthodox and he was summoned to Avignon by the Pope. He then hastily moved to Bavaria, where he was excommunicated, for his disobedience rather than for his ideas.

Peter Abelard and William of Ockham are the best-known medieval Nominalists. In modern terms the latter may be a Conceptualist rather than a Nominalist, since he views universals as ideas within the human mind, rather than mere words. A famous principle that arises from his refusal to accept the reality of universals is Ockham's Razor, which says we should reject every proposed entity (including universals) if it does not make a useful contribution to explanation and understanding. The slogan for this view is 'do not multiply entities beyond necessity', and its shortest statement might be 'keep it simple'. It is a guideline for the construction of any sort of theory.

William himself was cautious in his beliefs, and did not think we can prove either the existence of God or the immortality of the soul (which must rely on divine revelation). Like other Nominalists, he did not think a species was anything more than a group of individuals, and he criticized Aristotle's list of natural categories. He wasn't even sure whether or not the mind is separate from the body. Like Abelard, he denied the existence of both past and future, but unlike Abelard he also couldn't see how the present moment exists, so he concluded that time is unreal. His unusual view of morality was that we should not obey God because God is good, because it is the other way around, and what is good is settled by what God commands; God is more important than goodness. Our only moral duty is to love what God wants us to love.

Some of the issues which fascinated medieval philosophers may look remote from modern thought, but it is no accident that modern science emerged in Europe. They created an image of nature as ordered and capable of rational explanation, and insisted that scientific enquiry was not blasphemous but part of a thoughtful religion, which includes values as well as facts.

PHILOSOPHY FOR SCIENCE (1347-1650)

The great medieval theologians developed detailed and coherent philosophical theories, which combined Christian teaching with an account of nature derived from Aristotle. However, many of the leading thinkers came into conflict with the church, and the official doctrines became more rigidly orthodox, and not open to debate. In philosophy things moved slowly for the next century and a half, but the intellectual climate changed. The Renaissance in Italy began with art and architecture, but the 'humanist' movement placed greater emphasis on ancient Greek and Roman culture, and lost texts were rediscovered. The European discovery of the Americas was a huge stimulus toward bold thinking, because it revealed a whole new world which was unknown to the Greeks.

INTERLUDE (1347–1543)

When intellectual exploration is pushed to its limits, philosophy needs freedom of thought, but a religion needs a consensus.

Hence most of the major religions have experienced conflict between theologians attempting to construct doctrines which bind the believers together and scholars who want to explore the most difficult issues. The most inconvenient ideas usually came from scholars who had studied surviving philosophical texts from ancient Greece. Islam faced this problem in the tenth and eleventh centuries, when the discovery of ancient Greek texts (particularly of Aristotle) raised many challenging questions. After the publication of *The Incoherence of the Philosophers* by the highly influential theologian Abu Hamid al-Ghazzali (1058–1111), the world of orthodox Islam gradually moved against such enquiries.

The year 1347 saw a similar move in Christianity. Nicholas of Autrecourt was faced with an official list of 66 propositions which he was forbidden to teach, and he was forced to publicly burn his own books and recant. The University of Paris condemned the nominalist views of one of its own teachers, John of Mirecourt. By 1350 the University of Oxford was imposing the huge fine of five shillings for each time one of their graduate teachers diverged from the teachings of Aristotle, which was the new orthodoxy in philosophy. This is the emergence of what we now call Scholasticism, which is the very dogmatic and non-negotiable Christianized Aristotelianism that ruled the syllabuses of European universities for the next 250 years. Effectively, the type of free enquiry which was practised in ancient Greece and is studied in modern universities ground to a halt. The Inquisition already existed to fight against heresy, and philosophy withered away when faced with the power of such threats, which became stronger after Martin Luther's rebellious pronouncements in 1519. In 1559 Pope Paul IV launched the Index of Forbidden Books, and many subsequent classics of philosophy went straight onto this list. Although Christian theology lost much of its vitality because of such restrictions, one great thinker did emerge in Spain at the end of this period. Without challenging orthodoxy too severely, Francisco Suárez (1548–1617) explored, refined and criticized accepted Catholic theology, and was bold enough to eventually have some of his works banned. He also contributed important ideas that led to the development of international law.

Philosophy may have been largely reduced to a set of static doctrines, but the fifteenth century saw two huge developments that paved the way for the re-emergence of more critical thought. The simplest was the introduction into Europe in the 1450s of printed books by Johannes Gutenberg. Handwritten books were rare, expensive, and tightly controlled; printed books gradually became commonplace, cheaper, and much freer from restrictions. The less obvious development was the rediscovery, translation and publication of many ancient Greek texts, some of them hitherto unknown, and containing startling and challenging new ideas.

In 1417 the heroic Italian collector of manuscripts Poggio Bracciolini discovered in a German monastery the last existing copy of *On the Nature of Things* by Lucretius, a follower of Epicurus. This wonderful text says little about Epicurus' teaching on the primacy of pleasure, but gives extensive details of his atomism, and his doctrine of 'the swerve' in atomic movement (to allow humans freedom of choice), and raises some alarmingly bold questions about the nature and existence of the ancient gods. Between 1473 and 1620 this work was printed 37 times, and put epicurean ideas firmly on the map.

Before 1400 the only widely known work of Plato was a Latin translation of the first half of his *Timaeus*, but in Florence in the 1460s Marsilio Ficino translated Plato's complete works into Latin, and they soon appeared in printed versions. Ficino became the head of a revived version of Plato's Academy, and his pupil Giovanni Pico della Mirandola rose to be the most prominent intellectual in Italy. His *Oration on the Dignity of Man*, highly influenced by platonic thinking, was a provocative defence of new doctrines which helped to launch a renaissance in thought, despite achieving a swift ban by the church. The big revival of platonic thought in Florence did not, however, spread widely, and came to an end in the restrictive atmosphere that followed the Reformation.

It is a remarkable fact that while Plato was one of the greatest founders of Western philosophy, his influence was quite limited during the philosophical revival in the seventeenth and eighteenth centuries. Among ideas from the ancient world, what caught the attention of the new thinkers were doubts about the dogmatic authority of Aristotle, and the exciting rediscovery of ancient epicureanism, stoicism and scepticism. In the 1420s a

GIOVANNI PICO DALLA MIRANDOLA

Above: Pico della Mirandola led the new humanism, which encouraged careful study of ancient philosophy.

Latin translation of *Lives of the Philosophers* by Diogenes Laertius appeared. This work is a key source for ancient philosophy (other than our extensive texts by Plato and Aristotle). The work is full of dubious gossip, and its author was not a good philosopher, but the book contains long quotations from earlier texts, and what seem to be fairly accurate and neutral reports of what he had been reading. The work contains 82 lives, of varying length and interest, but the two which created the most excitement were the lives of Epicurus and of Zeno of Citium. Some lengthy letters by Epicurus were included in his life, giving details of the ethical side of epicureanism, which complemented the work of Lucretius to give a full picture of their doctrines. The life of Zeno of Citium had special importance, because the whole of the vast corpus of original stoic writings from the third century BCE had been lost (apart from a few quotations), but this short biography gave a very substantial account of the stoic movement and the man who originated it. Things move slowly in philosophy, but by the middle of the seventeenth century the rival options of stoicism and epicureanism had become an issue of major importance.

The third major rediscovery was the books of the second-century CE writer Sextus Empiricus, which appeared in Latin versions in the 1560s. These works (notably *Outlines of Pyrrhonism*) contained a sceptical onslaught on almost every belief it is possible to hold, and presented a clear, memorable and well-argued challenge to all the dogmatic beliefs which were held sacred in sixteenth-century Europe. As we shall see, it was attempts to confront these powerful sceptical arguments which launched modern philosophy.

In parallel to the tight grip of Aristotelian scholasticism, there also emerged the Humanist movement, exemplified by the great scholar Desiderius Erasmus, which took a much more tolerant attitude to the new classical texts which were appearing. Humanism was primarily an educational movement, encouraging the teaching of Greek, and a thoughtful and evaluative attitude to both the Bible and to secular texts. The humanists did not venture into serious metaphysics, which was a theological minefield, but did produce fresh political thinking, of which the most important came from Niccolò Machiavelli (1469–1527). His book *The Prince* still has the power to shock, because it so calmly and clearly lays out the best strategies for a successful prince of a small Italian state, which include a high degree of ruthlessness. It embodies the political concept of 'dirty hands' – that politicians may have to act according to practical principles which are clearly immoral in private life. For example, if you take over a new state, it is best to swiftly execute your enemies, and then be kind to the people for a while, because they will soon forget what you have done. The book explores few of the

Above: Political philosophy sprang to new life when Machiavelli proposed tough new ideas for ruling a state.

ideals that are central to modern works of political philosophy, but it set the agenda for new political thinking by going back to basics and trying to eliminate our prior prejudices on the subject.

An interesting diversion during this period was an enthusiasm for the writings of Hermes Trismegistus. This group of Greek texts was translated into Latin by Ficino in 1471 and their complex mixtures of mystical, magical, platonic and stoic ideas were attributed to ancient Egyptians, which gave them authority as some of the earliest philosophical writings. They established the tradition of Hermeticism, which still survives today, among those interested in supernatural occurrences. Pico della Mirandola was one enthusiast, and a notable later devotee was Giordano Bruno, who believed these old ideas along with the exciting new astronomical theories of Copernicus. Because his attachment to such ideas was resolute, Bruno was burned at the stake in Rome in 1600, and is sometimes seen as the second philosophical martyr (after Socrates). The authority of these hermetic texts collapsed in 1614, when Isaac Casaubon showed by linguistic analysis that they were actually written in around 300 CE.

Although rigorous philosophy had largely ceased, Michel de Montaigne (1533–92) was an important thinker in the relaxed mode found in later Stoics such as Seneca, Epictetus and Marcus Aurelius. He created the new genre of 'essays' (attempts), of which he wrote many, and his *Apology for Raimond Sebon* shows the strong influence of the recently discovered sceptical writings of Sextus Empiricus. In a world in which strong commitment to the dogmas of orthodoxy was expected, Montaigne professed, like Socrates, to know almost nothing, and hung a pendant around his neck asking *'Que sais-je?'* ('What do I know?') The sceptical questions which fill the writing of Sextus occur throughout his essays, which were widely read in Europe; the character of Shakespeare's Hamlet is infused with the spirit of Montaigne. His importance for European philosophy was that the extreme challenges of ancient scepticism became familiar, and a new age of bewildered speculation became unavoidable.

Above: Montaigne's insights into the problems of life were greatly influenced by his reading of ancient scepticism.

SCIENCE ARRIVES (1543–1620)

While the intellectual climate was changing a great deal because of the impact of printed books and the remarkable texts being resurrected from the distant past, some even more dramatic events were unfolding in the world of what we now call 'science' (then known as 'natural philosophy'). In 1543, the Polish monk Nicolaus Copernicus examined the available evidence from astronomy and wrote in his book *On the Revolutions of the Celestial Spheres* that it made much more sense if the Sun, rather than the Earth, was the centre of rotation for the moving heavenly bodies. His book was barely noticed at the time, but this changed when the Danish astronomer Tycho Brahe began to make very precise measurements of these heavenly movements, without the aid of a telescope. Such meticulous observations were a dramatic novelty in Western thought, quite apart from their consequences. Interest in Copernicus' heliocentric view of our solar system began to grow. A crucial next step was the recognition by the German Johannes Kepler that Copernicus' system would fit beautifully with Tycho Brahe's observations if the orbits of the planets were elliptical, rather than circular (which had been favoured by platonic prejudices about cosmic purity and order). Careful thinkers quickly recognized that the traditional Earth-centred cosmos endorsed by the Church was mistaken.

The invention in 1609 of the telescope, and its acquisition by the Italian scientist Galileo Galilei, soon clinched the matter, when he observed through his new instrument that moons were rotating around the planet Jupiter. This may not sound much to us, but it was one of the most dramatic observations ever made, because Galileo found himself staring in amazement at a new centre of rotation in the universe. He could actually *see* that not everything in the cosmos rotated around the Earth, so no further speculation was needed. This did not, however, save Galileo from conflict with the Church, and he ended his career under house arrest.

Above: New science, such as the revelation of Copernicus that we are not at the centre of the universe, greatly influenced philosophy.

The new revelations were not confined to cosmology. A second astounding book appeared in 1543. Andreas Vesalius was based at the University of Padua, and explored human anatomy by dissecting corpses. His *On the Fabric of the Human Body* not only introduced new precise and critical methods, but also remarkable diagrams to illustrate his findings. About a century later, the invention of the microscope revealed not only the smaller details of anatomy, but also the existence of tiny lifeforms which were hitherto unknown.

The modern scientific method was slowly emerging. Remarkable facts could be established with confidence, as long as problems were approached in a rigorous way. First, an objective and impersonal attitude must be adopted to observations, aiming at a prejudice-free consensus about them. It is then necessary to accurately measure items of interest, and compile the resulting data in an orderly way. Because the data is numerical, mathematics can then be applied to the findings. To concentrate investigations on a particular problem, an experiment with carefully controlled conditions must be set up. This experiment must be described carefully, and its findings must be published, so that other people can repeat the experiment if they don't trust the result. Critical evaluation by other researchers is to be encouraged.

These developments in cosmology, anatomy and methodology have their place in a history of philosophy, because of their implications. The first was the slow erosion of the Church of Rome as an authority on our knowledge of nature, because certain verses in the Bible were flatly contradicted by the new discoveries. The restrictions on freedom of thought which had held since 1347 were thereby loosened, making controversial philosophical discussion once again possible. The second was the challenge to the dogmatic authority of Aristotle.

Aristotle had achieved his status among Christian theologians because his metaphysics solved some of their difficulties. But he also had distinct views about natural philosophy, and these too had acquired dogmatic authority. He had argued against the atomism of Democritus, and so his view came to predominate: earthly nature is composed of four elements (earth, air, fire and water), and these are modes of an obscure basic 'prime matter', which is endlessly divisible. The key to understanding the natural world is to understand the 'essential nature' of each thing, by identifying the kinds that exist, and gradually developing full definitions of them, by observing their appearance and behaviour. Most famously, Aristotle explained things as much by their purposes as by what produced them. This teleological view of things meant that things only exist because of their purposes, and purposes particularly centred on human benefits, so that rain exists to foster crops, which exist to feed humans. He also believed that life developed spontaneously in locations such as decaying meat, which produced maggots. These widely accepted Aristotelian views – anti-atomism, essentialism and teleology – were swiftly challenged by the new science (and it was eventually proved that meat won't produce maggots if you prevent flies from laying eggs on it).

A key figure in this new challenge was Francis Bacon (1561–1626), who was an early fan of the experimental approach. He was a keen student of metaphysics, but his main interest was in the rejection of scholastic dogma about nature, which he laughed at as a statue which is worshipped, but never does anything. Perhaps his most important challenge was to teleological explanations; he saw that science must focus only on what Aristotle called 'efficient' causes, which create objects and lead up to events. This shift from explanation by purposes to explanation by prior causes and physical processes is one of the most important changes in all of Western thought. We usually explain natural phenomena now by what produced them, not by what they are for.

The new science encouraged empiricism (reliance on the senses), because experience was so obviously overruling mere theory, but Bacon took a mixed view of the matter. His famous analogy was that empiricists are like ants, collecting their data, while rationalists are like spiders, spinning theories from within themselves, but Bacon's preference was for the bee, which does both. His key thought was that nature must be manipulated to reveal its secrets, and the resulting data must be collected. Bacon tried to classify the various types of knowledge and offered an analysis of scientific methods,

Above: Francis Bacon's enthusiasm for experimental science launched and guided a new style of thinking.

focusing on induction (the gradual arrival at knowledge by the accumulation of facts).

RENÉ DESCARTES (1596–1650)

Descartes trained in scholastic metaphysics at a Jesuit college, but his vocation was for mathematics and science. His development of 'analytic geometry' was a major advance, because it meant that geometry could be reduced to algebra or arithmetic by plotting points on a system with x and y axes. This opened the way to the use of graphs and led to calculus. He also developed his own account of the workings of the cosmos, based on a system of 'vortexes' (that planetary orbits are whirlpools of matter, resulting from collisions).

Descartes might have confined himself to the sciences had it not been for Galileo's clash with the Inquisition, and also because of the deeply sceptical questions raised by the writings of Sextus Empiricus and Montaigne. He could have merely persevered with technical work, but instead in the 1630s he downed tools and in defence of what he was doing wrote two books, *Discourse on the Method* and *Meditations*, which are the foundations of modern philosophy. Without that decision it is possible that philosophy might have ended there, relegated to history as an outdated way to study the world. Instead, his books set the agenda for several centuries of creative theoretical thought.

Descartes' project was to start philosophy again from scratch. This meant confronting the toughest challenges of the sceptics, which suggested that we know almost nothing, to see whether they could be answered. This in itself was revolutionary, because it placed problems of knowledge rather than of existence at the centre of philosophy. The big question concerned *how* we can know anything, and *what* we know was given a lower priority.

Above: Modern philosophy began when René Descartes took it back to basics, to give a rational grounding for science.

His train of thought (in *Meditations*) starts with two sceptical suggestions – that his mind may be generating a delusional world, or that some outside force is giving him false experiences. That is, he might be dreaming (with exceptional vividness), or he might be in virtual reality (generated by an 'evil demon'). Aristotle actually laughed at such suggestions, but Descartes takes them very seriously, because he is seeking certainty, and you are not certain of something if you are aware of even the faintest chance that you might be wrong.

Descartes is bewildered by such far-reaching doubts, but then offers a glimmer of an escape – that if he is in a state of doubt, then he is *certainly* doubting. Hence he arrives at the famous *cogito ergo sum* (I am thinking, therefore I exist). The idea occurs in the writings of Augustine, but in Descartes it had revolutionary significance, because from now on philosophy increasingly focused on the mind of the person who thought or knew something, rather than on the content of what they knew. The Cogito argument has its critics, who often ask whether thinking proves that there is a stable self which exists over time, but no one can doubt that existence is a certainty if thinking is occurring.

Descartes' next move was a more controversial one, because he revived the ontological argument for God's existence put forward by Anselm but rejected by Aquinas. This is the argument which uses the pure concept of God to prove that God exists. Descartes' version starts from the definition of God as 'a supremely perfect being', which is more absolute than Anselm's reliance on the limits of our ability to conceive such a thing. The argument quickly proceeds to his belief that existence is one of God's perfections, which implies that God necessarily exists. The reason for this move is to show that there is a perfect God who will protect us from the delusions of dreams or evil demons, and hence offer a guarantee that at least some of our basic knowledge is certain.

However, Descartes knows that we can be wrong about some things, so some further non-divine criterion is needed to provide a foundation for human knowledge. His concept of a 'supremely perfect being' is taken to be 'innate' within his mind – that is, the idea is directly obvious, and has not resulted from prior experiences. He asserts that we have many such ideas, found in geometry and the necessities of ordinary life, and we can draw interesting inference from them, by 'the natural light of reason'. We now see the existence of innate ideas as basic to the Rationalist school of philosophy, because it offers a route to truth which doesn't rely on experience, about which the sceptics have made us suspicious.

Descartes also explicitly argued against the sense-based empiricist view of knowledge. He gives the striking example of a wax candle, which is taken to be wax because of the appropriate experiences it causes in our five senses. However, he says, if you melt a wax candle, you have a puddle of hot wax which gives us quite different experiences from those given us by the solid candle – and yet we still think we are experiencing wax. His conclusion from this is that our knowledge that it is wax does not come from our experiences, but from our subsequent *judgement* of the experiences. Hence knowledge is primarily a matter for the intellect, and not for the senses, thus reinforcing his rationalist view of knowledge. Rational knowledge must depend on our ability to directly grasp certain truths, so Descartes places his greatest confidence in judgements which are 'clear and distinct'. His *Discourse on the Method* set out more detailed guidelines for how we can double check and test our judgements to maximize their chances of success. Near the end of *Meditations* it is this calm and rational assessment of the evidence which offers a secure denial of the sceptical claim that normal sense experience may be wrong, or that our erratic dreams might be really happening.

Descartes' Cogito argument offers the claim that the existence of the mind is necessary and certain for us, even when the physical world (which includes our own bodies) is thrown into doubt by scepticism. This leads him to the claim that the mind and the body must be quite separate entities (a view now known as 'substance dualism'), and he offers further arguments to support his view. The body is obviously made up of parts, but the mind forms a perfect unity. Also the body clearly exists in space, but we have no sense at all that our thoughts occupy a specific physical volume, since they can be universal or infinite in character. This aspect of Descartes' work soon provoked responses from other thinkers, and launched what we now call the 'philosophy of mind'.

Some of Descartes' scientific ideas also had an influence on philosophy. He was the first scientist to talk about the 'laws of nature', obviously influenced by the fact that natural regularities were beginning to be expressed in equations, and that Galileo famously wrote that 'the book of nature is written in mathematics'. The concept of laws of nature started out as the divine commands of God which rule the world, but gradually acquired an apparent authority of their own, so that we now think of nature as being controlled by such laws, which scientists are trying to identify.

Descartes also recognized that Aristotle's concept of matter was inadequate for the new thinking, and offered the idea that matter is defined simply by the space which it occupies. His proposal gained few supporters (since the space might be hollow), but provoked thinking about how philosophers should conceive of the basics of the physical world, leading many modern philosophers to the study of quantum theory. He was also famous for his claim that animals are quite incapable of reason, on the grounds that they cannot speak, and that they should be best understood as machines (in contrast to humans, whose being includes a mind).

Descartes offered no views on theology, politics, ethics, aesthetics or logic, but his thinking is strikingly systematic, and immediately captivated his contemporaries because it is so clear, raises so many new problems, and is supported at each stage by reasons for what he believes. Part of his huge influence came from his brave decision to invite criticisms of his *Meditations* before they were even published. He circulated the manuscript to the greatest thinkers in Paris and they each wrote objections to the work, to which the author wrote his replies. The *Meditations* were then published complete with objections and replies, and thus launched both a system and a debate about the system. Descartes founded modern philosophy as much by this invitation to freely discuss the ideas as by the nature of the ideas themselves.

CHAPTER 6

PHILOSOPHY FROM EXPERIENCE (1640-1720)

Descartes wrote his philosophical works in order to defend the newly emerging science by giving it rational and religious foundations. Because he started from extreme scepticism, he distrusted the senses, which were only rescued from doubt by 'the natural light of reason'. Hence we now see him as a rationalist philosopher. However, it seemed obvious that the new science was going to be an empirical activity, dependent on careful observations. Although experiments must be evaluated by reason, the truth was more closely connected to what was observed than to what was thought about the observations.

The empiricist tradition from the ancient world was familiar in the seventeenth century, because most of the classic texts were now available in translation – so Epicureans took sense experience to be almost infallible, and Stoics relied on senses if they were given full attention and critical evaluation. The scientists themselves began to make breakthroughs when they observed physical events more carefully. Tycho Brahe's meticulous observations led to acceptance of the Earth's orbit around the Sun, and Galileo became famous for using telescope observations to oppose the dogmas of the church. The microscope was having an equally dramatic impact. Hence it is not surprising that many of the responses to Descartes were empirical in emphasis. Two of the Objections to his *Meditations* were written by the empiricists Thomas Hobbes and Pierre Gassendi.

THOMAS HOBBES (1588–1679)

Hobbes was led into philosophy by his fluency in Greek and wide reading of ancient texts. He rebelled against the rigid scholasticism of Oxford University and was struck by the more materialistic views of the Epicureans and Stoics, and the beautiful geometry of Euclid. He is best known for his political philosophy, but his thought is wide-ranging, and based on systematic metaphysics.

His ontology (basic views of being) was nominalist and materialist – that is, he saw reality as entirely consisting of physical objects, and so all talk of the properties of objects, or their essences, or general truths about them, were simply a matter of words. Like the Greeks, Hobbes loved definitions, but for him the definitions of physical things consisted only of what had caused them; like the new scientists, he saw 'efficient' cause as the only significant one of Aristotle's four different types. The formal (essential) cause, the material cause and the final (teleological) cause could be ignored. A thing's efficient cause is the events that lead up to it. Since nothing more can be observed than these events, Hobbes defined cause as a close connection between events which results in a change. Change is simply a movement in matter, triggered by a driving force (conatus) in nature, and movement is merely a change of place. In this way Hobbes is a reductive physicalist. The mysterious causes are reduced to events, and eventually to simple change of place. Hence all of reality can be reduced to nothing more than matter changing its location, which is a view of reality close to the atomism of Democritus and Epicurus.

Like his ancient predecessors, Hobbes applied his materialist reduction to the human mind, which is nothing more than movements inside our heads. Given that rather shocking view (for its time), it is not surprising that he was sceptical about religion. He took our image of God to be a mere collection of impressive human attributes, and immortality to be based on unsupported rumours, which is only believed because of our ignorance and fear of death. He saw formal religions as simply legalized versions of this fear of unknown powers. In short,

Above: Thomas Hobbes held the controversial views that reality is entirely physical, morality is just contracts between people, and religion is false.

Hobbes was an atheist, and hence a very controversial figure, who was lucky to survive into old age.

As we would expect, Hobbes had no time for free will, which

he explains by our inability to experience whatever causes our choices. We think our choices could have been different, because we are unaware of the mental movements that produced them. He challenges anyone (even a non-materialist) to say what act of will produces each act of will. If acts of will do not result from acts of will, then we do not control them. He doesn't even believe there is such a thing as the will, because it reduces simply to the last desire before an action. He compares supposedly free actions to water running down a hill, which seems to move freely, but has to travel along a certain route.

Hobbes was a realist about the external world. We are not trapped in private experiences, because we can see which of them is reliable and which unreliable. When we look in a mirror, it is obvious which is the image and which is the reality. When we dream, it is obvious that dreams are full of absurdities, but waking life is consistent and can be explained. Hence he found little interest in the broad scepticism which troubled Descartes. He also said we should be cautious about theories of what is possible, because it may be easy to imagine some bizarre possible event, but you also have to imagine how the event could come about, which is much more difficult.

He took an interest in the old problem of what defines an object, and how we can pick one out, especially when it changes over time. On the one hand a part of an object must move when the whole object moves, but on the other we can think of scattered parts (such as a dismantled clock) as a single object. The Greeks had used the example of the Ship of Theseus, which seems to remain the same ship even when its planks are replaced as it ages, as a test case for the problem. Hobbes introduced a delightful variant of this. Suppose someone kept the discarded planks, and built a new ship of them once they had a complete set. You would then have two ships, one of fresh planks and the other of original planks, each a good candidate for being the unique Ship of Theseus. Modern discussions of the puzzle of how to identify something with changing parts nearly always focus on Hobbes' example.

Hobbes was unusual in showing the moral principles implied by his own metaphysics. He rejected the teleological explanations of Aristotle, so not only is there no purpose in nature, there is no ultimate purpose in human life either. All that matters in life is our desires, and how to fulfil them. He dismissed the virtues as mere strategies for mutual benefit, reduced pure goodness to whatever pleases us, and said even God's goodness is nothing more than supposed kindness to humanity. The key to morality is how to satisfy our desires in a social setting, and that is a matter of making contracts with other people.

In his great work *Leviathan* he examines the dependence of our moral lives on contracts (an idea first discussed in Plato's *Republic*). The first question is why people would make contracts, and his famous answer is that without a society humans are naturally warlike, and so life is 'solitary, poor, nasty, brutish and short'. Hence we must make agreements in order to avoid such misery. The problem is that simultaneous exchange of favours is fine, but if the returned favour comes later, why bother? Once you have received a favour, where's the benefit in repaying it? You might hope for future favours, or fear retaliation, but basically everyone is motivated to break contracts if they can get away with it.

Above: Thomas Hobbes' *Leviathan* argued that a good society just needs to enforce the agreements made between people.

At this point his theory of individual morality expands into a political theory. To make contracts people need to be roughly equal (because otherwise the strong can take from the weak without negotiation). People must also control something which they can offer in negotiation, which implies citizens who are reasonably free. All injustice is the breaking of a contract, so the prime aim of the state is to ensure that this doesn't happen. Hobbes rejected the idea of punishment as traditional revenge, and said its only aim was to prevent people from being unjust. Hence the solution to his main problem is that a strong authority must control society, with the enforcement of agreements as almost its only power. Hobbes preferred a traditional monarch in the role, because monarchs were seen as having an absolute authority, often supported by religious doctrines.

Hobbes seems to be defending tyranny, but there is a crucial further step in his argument. If all social interaction is a matter of agreements and contracts, then the status of the absolute authority must also result from the agreement of the people. This introduces the hugely influential idea of a social contract. Most states in the Europe of his time were ruled by hereditary monarchs, whose authority (or 'sovereignty') resulted from tradition and the decree of God. Hobbes' theory of contractual morality needed sovereignty to come from the people. This did not mean a country was controlled by its people, because their rights were handed over to the sovereign power, but it meant that a monarch needed popular support, which was likely to be lost if the contracts between citizens were not respected. For Hobbes the law was merely a tool for appropriate enforcement, so he rejected the doctrine of natural law in favour of 'positive' law (which just consists of rules we find convenient).

The influence of Hobbes is often underestimated. He was the first important philosopher in the English language, but he also greatly influenced Spinoza and Rousseau. He launched modern political philosophy, which increasingly focused on rights, he gave expression to scepticism about religion, and he revealed the implications of empiricism. His thinking was controversial, but it endured.

JOHN LOCKE (1632–1704)

Locke spent most of his career at Oxford University, having grown up during the English Civil War, which (as with Hobbes) greatly influenced his political thinking. He saw a direct link between his empiricist philosophy and the new science, and modestly described himself as an 'under-labourer' in the enterprise. His major work, *An Essay Concerning Human Understanding*, was published three years after Isaac Newton's publication of the law of gravity. Locke was an empiricist, but had no sympathy with the atheism and materialism of Hobbes.

Locke began the *Essay* with an attack on what he saw as the key belief of rationalists like Descartes – that the mind contains innate ideas. Rationalists don't ignore experience, but they rely on a foundation of self-evident truths and concepts which are born in us, or emerge by a process of pure reason. The best-known examples are the concept of God, the basic ideas of mathematics, and the rational principles which can be applied to them. Locke demanded evidence for the innateness of an idea. How do we tell whether the idea of a triangle is born within us, or is somehow extracted from experience? Descartes said we have ideas of an infinity of triangles, but only experience a few of them, which implies innateness. But how do we tell whether the numerous triangles are innate, or created by imagination when required? Locke concludes that innate ideas are either trivial (if they are just potential thoughts) or absurd (if we make huge claims about the knowledge hidden in infants).

Without innate ideas, Locke's starting point is an empty mind (a 'tabula rasa', or blank page) which is merely receptive to experiences. Locke's ontology (his basic theories of what exists) must therefore be assembled entirely from experiences. He was familiar with the ideas of traditional scholastic metaphysics (such as substances, essences, universals and categories), but assessed them according to whether they were supported by evidence.

The great idea of Being is nothing more than our experiences, and Locke declared himself to be a nominalist, meaning that reality consists purely of objects,

Above: John Locke built a system based wholly on experience, which aimed to support the thinking of scientists.

so there are no further general facts, and there are no universal properties that exist, other than as features of objects. Hence nature must be explained by means of these objects. This is close to Aristotle's view, but that relied on the idea that each object has an essential nature, which we identify by means of the category into which the object falls. However, for Locke the evidence which might reveal essential natures and precise categories was not at all clear.

He felt that categorizing the world was just a convenient verbal simplification. He observed, for example, that species can merge into one another, and that no precise definition of an animal species will fit every single one of its members, since there are many deformities at birth. He divided essences into 'nominal' and 'real', where the nominal essence is the verbal summary of the surface properties. The real essence is the hidden nature of a thing, with which we have no contact. Essentialists say that if you know the real essence of a thing you can predict its properties and behaviour, but Locke thought such knowledge was forever beyond us. One consequence of this is that Locke was quite pessimistic about the future prospects for science (and would have been astounded at what has since been achieved).

Traditional metaphysicians had further worries about how we can individuate (pick out) an object, and how we can know its identity over time. Locke's solution was that we can only know the thing's location in space and time, but that is enough to fix its individuality since no two objects can share a location, and we can identify it over time by specifying its origin, because that is unique to each object, and it can then be tracked to the present moment. This is attractively simple and properly empirical, but it ignores the Ship of Theseus problem (of an object changing its parts) which had bothered Hobbes.

Locke was not interested in scepticism or relativism, but believed that secure empirical knowledge is possible. Our mind, having started as a *tabula rasa*, is filled with ideas, all of which result directly or indirectly from experience. He gives an explanation of language in this way, because our words are said to be signs which indicate the ideas. This theory of the meanings of words launches the Philosophy of Language, which is a major area in modern philosophy. Locke leaves many questions unanswered about how the ideas are organized and filtered to produce knowledge, but he noticed that ideas tend to form connections, as when the sight of a room can remind us of a person who has died in it, for example.

Locke emphasized an important distinction about the qualities of objects. Some qualities, such as shape, size, weight, hardness and movement, are supported by more than one sense (such as shape being both felt and seen). On those we would expect everyone to agree, but other qualities seem to depend on one sense alone (such as colour and taste), and often produce disagreement between people. The first group contains the 'primary' qualities, and the second group the 'secondary' qualities. The former seem to be objective and capable of measurement, while the latter are more personal and subjective (even if they are informative). The importance of this distinction is that science relies almost entirely on the objective and measurable primary qualities. As we shall see, this distinction, which offers philosophical support for science, became controversial among philosophers and provoked increasingly complex debates.

To illustrate the limitations of secondary qualities, Locke introduced his famous problem of 'inverted qualia' (swapped qualities). If two people in a garden are looking at violets and orange marigolds, they will assume that they are having the same experiences of the colours – but how can they be sure? If one person's brain had swapped qualities (seeing violets as orange and marigolds as violet) the two people would agree on the words 'violet' and 'orange', never realizing that their experiences were not the same. A hundred years later it was discovered that many people actually are colour-blind, but had failed to realize it. This is a problem which doesn't seem to arise for primary qualities.

Locke was impressed by the special unity seen in the mind, but not in the body, so he believed (like Descartes) that they are quite different substances. He also accepted God's existence, mainly because the existence we experience only seems possible if there is Eternal Being. Because he took the mind to be separable from the body, Locke became intrigued with the puzzle of how personal identity is retained if they come apart. For example, if the consciousness of a prince were transferred into the body of a cobbler, we would assume that he was still the prince, with all his responsibilities. But if a man's mind were transferred into a pig, we wouldn't say the pig had become a man.

This led Locke to introduce an important distinction, between a 'person' and a 'human being'. The person is a fully developed consciousness, involving reason, memory and self-awareness. Hence an infant or a senile old person might count as a human being, but not be accepted as a person. The law focuses on persons, because they can be held responsible, and identity over time depends on the person (for example the prince). Locke offered the theory that personal identity over time consists of long stretches of memory. This idea opened up a whole new topic in philosophy and it remains a live issue, with several rival theories.

In his *Second Treatise on Government* Locke produced an important account of politics. He felt that the absolute monarchy favoured by Hobbes was too dangerous. Locke offered instead the idea that private property is what protects our rights against tyrants, and so the protection of property is the foundation of social justice. Since property can be stolen, his theory needed an account of just ownership, and this derived from the natural ownership of the results of a person's labour. If fruit grows on a tree in a state of nature it has no owner, but if someone climbs the tree and picks it, they are the natural owner of the fruit, because of the effort involved. A person can become the owner of a piece of unwanted land if they cultivate it to produce crops. Locke presumes that human beings own the earth, that people own their own bodies, and that property can be inherited within a family. His commitment to property is so strong that a soldier may be obliged to die, but never to hand over his property. There are constraints on this method of ownership, because Locke has a sense of natural justice. People may acquire land by their labour, but never more land than they need, and the land must not then be wasted.

It follows from this account of justice that all people are naturally equal and deserving of respect, because they can all achieve ownership through labour. Hence Locke endorsed Hobbes' powerful new idea of a social contract, that the sovereignty of a state must arise from the will of the people, and he began to explore some of the problems with the theory. The people can't reaffirm their will every day, so the founding of a society must be democratic, but after that it is the law and the tax system which embody the popular will.

Freedom in a society is not doing whatever you like, but living by the laws which have been communally agreed. This means that rebellions can be justified if the law very obviously departs from what the people want, and especially if the law contradicts the right to property. The other problem is that new members of a society, by birth or from abroad, have had no say in the popular will. Locke says there is 'tacit consent' to the society if you partake of its benefits (such as travelling on its roads), but Hume later said that is like tacitly agreeing to a sea voyage when you have been carried onto the ship while asleep.

GEORGE BERKELEY (1684–1753)

Berkeley was a church minister who became a bishop in Ireland, but he adopted a strong version of empiricism, and pursued it to a surprising conclusion. Locke was a realist, and took it that the ideas produced by experience (at least of the primary qualities) accurately represent reality. But Berkeley was aware of the scepticism that troubled Descartes, and it is obvious that we can doubt whether our ideas really do represent things successfully. Empiricism threatens to cut us off from reality, and thus destroy human knowledge.

We might try saying that we experience reality directly, rather than via the representations by ideas, but Berkeley thought the sceptical arguments were too strong for that. The so-called secondary qualities are quite unreliable. If you plunge a hot hand and a cold hand into tepid water, they give different experiences. Our feet may look large to us, but an insect's feet look large to the insect. And even solidity is relative to how strong you are, so the primary qualities cannot be trusted either, and Locke's primary/secondary distinction is false. The realist view says that things stay roughly the same, but we know that our experiences of them change continually, as we get closer to them, or it gets dark. Our five senses each give a quite different impression of reality, so which one is telling the truth? Empiricists can trust their experiences, but should not trust some 'reality' said to be hidden behind them.

Berkeley's solution to all of these doubts was drastic: what we should say is that our experiences *are* reality. Thus from a rather scientific and empirical starting point, Berkeley embraced 'idealism' (the view that reality consists entirely of mental events). He found support for his view when he considered the traditional ideas that each object is a 'substance' to which properties attach, that the substance has an 'essential nature', and that the world is made of 'matter', which produces its appearances. None of these ideas explain anything about the world, so they can all be abandoned. We are left with objects as bundles of properties, and the properties

Dʳ GEORGE BERKELE
Biſhop of Cloyne.

Above: George Berkeley relied on experience, but for him it only proved our ideas, and not the unknowable external world.

are sensations in our minds. His famous slogan for this was that 'to exist is to be perceived'.

A further step in Berkeley's thought is that the empirical principle must be applied to our thinking as well as to our sensations. In the case of geometry, we are asked to believe in the abstract idea of a triangle, with an infinity of possible shapes and sizes, but such a thing is unthinkable. Every attempt to think of the general triangle just produces one particular triangle. Hence these universal abstract objects are non-existent, and should be forgotten. Geometry is just memories of a multitude of individual perceptions, and the generalizations about them are a mere matter of words. Like Locke, Berkeley was a Nominalist about such things.

Berkeley's empirical idealism faces two large problems. The first is what happens to objects, such as his desk, when he is not experiencing them? Is failure to be perceived a failure to exist? This divides into two problems: what if some other person is experiencing the desk, and what if no one at all is experiencing the desk? Berkeley asserts his confidence that there are other minds than his own, because he experiences them in conversation. He also wonders whether we can accept the desk as a *possibility* for perception, even when it is not perceived. When no one at all perceives the desk, Berkeley turns to the eternal perceptions of God as the guarantee of an enduring ideal reality. The need for such a guarantee gives us a reason to believe in God, though he also agrees with the Design Argument (that the orderliness of reality implies a Designer). This is an obvious weak point in his theory, because God can be doubted, and the reason for believing in other minds is also a reason to simply believe in the desk. Without some way, however, to reinforce belief in the enduring nature of reality, Berkeley would be faced with solipsism – the view that nothing exists except my *own* mind. After a bold start, the new empiricism was beginning to waver.

CHAPTER 7

PHILOSOPHY FROM REASON (1640-1720)

There is no precise way to divide the history of philosophy into datable periods. The term 'medieval' is used for the many centuries between the first emergence of Christianity and about 1400, with an early and a later period. The Renaissance, a golden age for the visual arts but a quiet one in philosophy, is dated from about 1400 until 1600. An event of great importance during that period was the discovery of the Americas by Europeans in 1492. Among its consequences was a realization that this had never been achieved by the awe-inspiring ancient Greeks and Romans, which led to a gradual decline in the authority of those cultures.

THE ENLIGHTENMENT

The period from 1600 to 1800 was long known as the Age of Reason, but is now usually referred to as the Enlightenment (or more recently as the Early Modern period). For philosophers, five events outside philosophy were of major importance. In 1610,

Galileo published his discovery of the rotation of the moons of Jupiter, which implied that human beings are not at the centre of the universe; in 1687, Newton published his law of gravity in his book *Philosophiæ Naturalis Principia Mathematica* (*Mathematical Principles of Natural Philosophy*); in 1649 the English parliament executed their own king; in 1776 the American colonies declared their independence; and in 1789 the people of France overthrew their entire government. These events resulted from new political thinking, and in turn stimulated very different political ideas after 1800.

Above: Enlightenment thinkers believed that all truths would gradually emerge if our discussions were rational.

The influence of Newton was of a different type. His book was the culmination of a revised idea of the solar system, but the amazing new idea was that all gravitational attraction (of apples or of planets) could be explained and predicted by a single short equation: $F = G(m_1 m_2/d^2)$; that is, the force F between two objects m_1 and m_2 equals their two masses multiplied together, then divided by the square of the distance between them (d), all multiplied by the constant strength of gravity (G). Nowadays we are familiar with scientific equations, but thinkers of Newton's time were inspired by the novelty of an idea which was so simple and yet so powerful. It resulted in great excitement about the possibilities of science, and a new high status for mathematics (of which the main uses so far had been for business book-keeping, surveying and gambling).

There is an obvious connection between scientific progress and empiricism, and the supremacy of mathematics had a similar role for rationalist philosophy. Both Descartes and Leibniz were great mathematicians as well as philosophers, and the proofs of mathematics and the theorems of Euclid's geometry (built up from a few minimal assumptions) were models for a way in which a rational system of thought might be constructed. Formal logic made no progress beyond Aristotle during the Enlightenment, but there was a keen interest in the nature of reason, and attempts to identify the minimal 'laws of thought' on which it is based.

There slowly emerged during this period an enormous confidence that a rational approach could solve almost any problem. The issues of religion, morality and politics were studied, and bold attempts made to justify high ideals in terms of a few basic assumptions. In modern times the idea of the Enlightenment is associated with this supreme faith in reason, which has led to strong disagreements.

BARUCH SPINOZA (1632–77)

Spinoza is often ranked with Socrates as one of the great heroes of Western philosophy because of his humble, single-minded and thoroughly rational contribution to the subject. He was expelled from the Amsterdam Jewish community as a young man, and earned a lonely and modest living while pursuing philosophy. His principle work, *Ethics*, only published after his early death, is set out with orderly precision, using Euclid's geometry as his model.

His starting point was the troublesome dualist theory of mind of Descartes. This proposed two basic and very different substances, mind and matter, but left the problem of how the mind and the brain could influence one another. If a ghost can walk through a wall, how can a ghost build a wall? For Hobbes there was no problem, because the mind is just movement of matter. Spinoza agreed that merging mind and matter is the only solution, but not by eliminating the mind in this way. Spinoza therefore proposed that reality contains

Above: Spinoza was a highly independent thinker, who said that nature, mind and God are all just aspects of a single substance.

one single substance, which has an infinity of features. The mind is the mental aspect of this substance, and the brain is its material aspect.

The one substance with an infinity of features and a mental aspect obviously exists, and can be identified with God. Hence Spinoza affirmed that God and Nature are one unified thing (the view we call 'pantheism'), with two distinct modes of being. Spinoza's concept of God is a long way from that of orthodox religions, which tend to have human attributes such as compassion, wisdom and moral motivation. Spinoza joked that a triangle's god would be perfectly triangular, so we mustn't read humanity into God, which he takes to be a remote and unlovable source of law and power, with no further purpose beyond existence. Immortality after death is merely reabsorption into the single substance, and God has no need to perform miracles. Because of such views, many later thinkers took Spinoza to be an atheist (which he would certainly have denied).

Like Hobbes, Spinoza did not believe in free will. Since there is only one substance, nothing can step outside of Nature to produce independent causes of actions (as true free will is supposed to do). We have invented the idea that we have total freedom simply because we are unaware of where our decisions come from. More surprisingly, Spinoza says that God is in the same position, since there is just a single ongoing system of causes, which means that the whole of reality is pre-determined, and everything must be the way it is (the doctrine we now call 'determinism'). The nearest we get to full freedom is when we know that our actions arise from our own essential nature, which means arising from our reason (an idea Spinoza inherited from the Stoics).

Although Spinoza gives reason central importance in our lives, he does not believe (as Descartes did) in a fixed Ego or Self, and for him the essence of a human being is the 'conatus', the combination of will and appetite which promotes our own existence and benefits. The traditional view was that a human is a tangle of essentially selfish and dangerous emotions, which must be controlled by reason. Spinoza, however, says we must not condemn this essential selfish drive, but accept it. Reason (which sees things 'from the point of view of eternity') has a supreme value, but it is rational to acknowledge selfish motivation, provided we ensure that it does not become stupid and destructive.

Spinoza agreed with Hobbes that the whole of morality can be derived from the rational selfishness of each individual. He ignored the role of contracts, but saw goodness as nothing more than success for each individual, largely understood as pleasure and avoidance of pain, and saw the virtues as mere strategies for achieving this. A good life, for Spinoza, was a joyful life. He was in favour of helping people in trouble, but he disliked the emotion of pity, which is an unpleasant experience, and not needed in the motivation of good actions. The more healthy and productive emotions are not mere feelings, but have an intellectual content, and are expressions of attitudes to things. Hence his morality is a highly rational one, and he was a leader in creating the new Age of Reason, with its optimism about order and progress, and its faith that if we are all rational our beliefs will converge on truth and wisdom.

The influence of the Stoics can be seen again in Spinoza's three-stage account of knowledge. He writes of the 'adequacy' of a belief, which indicates how securely it is known. The main aim is to achieve understanding, rather than to know items of information, and he sees this as a broad relationship among our beliefs, which only make sense in relation to one another (a 'holistic' view), and which are assessed by their rational coherence. The lowest level is not reliable, and involves either random experiences and imagination, or verbal reports (which are not true ideas, but merely represent them). The second level is much more secure, and is derived from reasoning about experience, using evaluated and adequate ideas of things, and the developed principles of understanding which we all share. At this level we see the necessity in things, and begin to grasp the essence of nature (which is equivalent to grasping the mind of God). It is a hallmark of the second level that we have knowledge, and also know that we have it. The highest level of knowledge, called 'intuition', may be too difficult for human beings, and involves direct insight into reality, leading to a vision of how things must be. Spinoza holds the unusual view that the fully or adequately grasped truth is its own justification, and doesn't need supporting evidence.

As so often with the major figures in philosophy, there is a clear rational progress from Spinoza's metaphysics to his ethics, and thus to his political theories. A person is essentially a drive to survive, with hidden motives which all aim at self-interest, and achieve their greatest success when they are focused by reason. The aim of life is to be pain-free and joyful, and achieve the highest possible level of understanding. The self-interested character of this does not, however, lead to competition and hostility, but to a recognition that rational people all have the same interests, and should work together to achieve them. Spinoza's political ideals are close to those of a modern liberal democracy.

He rejected the solution of Hobbes to the problem of social freedom, which was to agree on the powers of an absolute monarch, able to enforce contracts between citizens. Spinoza could see the obvious danger if the social contract (the agreement of the people) was used to install a monarch, because it was then difficult for the people to retain any control, or to get rid of a bad monarch. Monarchs are often both stubborn and irrational. Hobbes defended a natural right to self-preservation, but Spinoza went much further, saying that we have a natural right to fulfil all of our desires. Spinoza's highest ideals for a civilized and successful society were free speech and tolerance of dissenters, which are both essential principles in a rational community. A state is only successful if the citizens fully co-operate with the laws, and that only happens if the laws are rational, and not just firmly enforced. The greatest danger to a state, he says, is its own citizens, when they lose faith in the reasonableness of their social system.

Unsurprisingly, he thought it important that a state should keep religion under control, and make the major decisions about communal religion (even though dissent is tolerated). His reason is that the law must have supreme authority, and religions lay claim to a higher authority, which might see itself as above the law. Spinoza was ahead of his time in denouncing slavery. The aim of a society is that all persons should be free to express their own personal desires and aims, and so his objection to slavery was not its cruelty, but the fact that slaves are only able to pursue the desires of their owners. The political thinking of Spinoza implies a democracy in which the individual rights of each citizen have the highest importance, and in which there is a minimum of restriction on the lifestyle of each person, other than by laws that are universally agreed.

GOTTFRIED LEIBNIZ (1646-1716)

A person of exceptional all-round abilities, Leibniz launched the important German philosophical tradition. He spent most of his career employed at the court of Hanover, but became famous for his wide correspondence with the major intellectuals of his time. In addition to his philosophy, he created calculus – the mathematics of things which continuously change. He wrote a vast amount, of which most was unpublished in his lifetime, the best-known work being *Monadology* (1715), a short summary of his views.

At a time when progress in science was encouraging empiricist philosophers, Leibniz kept faith with the traditional Aristotelian approach to metaphysics and was interested in substances and essences, and the possible revelations of pure reason. However, he was aware that times had changed, and science was producing better accounts of nature, by means of experiments, detailed observations, and the application of mathematics. He was particularly struck by the window into the hidden structure of matter offered by the microscope. Unlike Locke, Leibniz did not see metaphysics as an extension of science, but as an important and separate area of thought. He had little to say about ethics or politics, but his system of thought is famous for its consistency and thoroughness.

For Leibniz the most important idea emerging in science was the concept of a 'force'. Newton's Laws of Motion concern forces, and include the law that 'every action has an equal and opposite reaction'. This implies a passive type of force, as a wall resists when

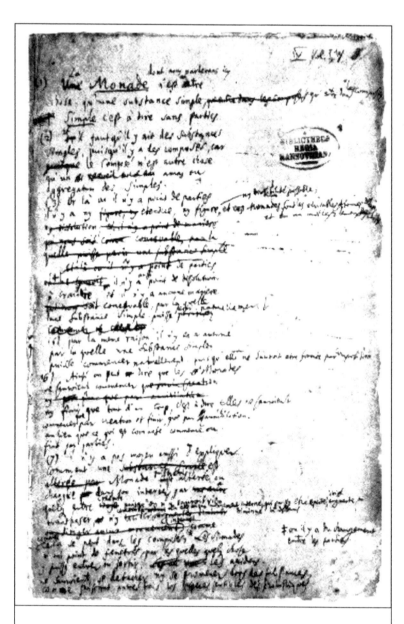

Above: The *Monadology* of Leibniz summarizes his account of how reality is built on a hive mind-like foundation.

pushed. There are also active forces in nature, seen in growth, the weather and the movement of planets. So a metaphysical account of matter must explain active and passive forces, which are its foundation.

Leibniz said the only possible origin of force is a mind, since mere matter seems incapable of producing activity. By combining that view with the observation through microscopes that there are lifeforms too small to see with the naked eye, he concluded that life and mind are the two essential foundations of the physical world. The Epicureans claimed that matter is made of tiny unsplittable particles (atoms), because it would be absurd if the splitting of matter could go on forever (which would eventually arrive at nothing). Leibniz agreed with this, but said that because atoms bounce off one another and make connections they must have parts, and parts can be separated, and hence no material particle could ever be a perfect atom. An unsplittable atom must have perfect unity, and the only thing which has perfect unity (as Descartes had observed) is a mind. Hence Leibniz proposed a different type of atoms, which he called 'monads'. These basic components of nature are not lifeless particles, but have the active power and unity of living minds. Each monad is a substance, so Leibniz believed in an infinity of substances (where Descartes believed in two, and Spinoza in one).

Leibniz was mocked at the time for his theory, and it has few modern fans, but it is important to understand his claim correctly. He never made the simple assertion that reality is made of minds, but always referred to his monads as 'mind-like'. He understood the major features of a mind to be will, memory, perception and appetite, and of these he only needed something like appetite and

Above: Leibniz was an awesome mathematician and scholar, and the creator of a complex and coherent rational system.

perception to explain the basic sources of active and passive natural forces. So a basic monad has no will or memory, and hence no independent thought.

Leibniz also applied to monads an important observation about our own minds. He pointed out that if you look at a fine grid of blue and yellow dots and gradually retreat from it, there comes a point where it will look green. This reveals that our perceptions are not what they seem, and are composed of fine ingredients of which we are barely conscious. He decided that consciousness comes in degrees, and that the high level of human consciousness is assembled from parts, some of which are not conscious at all. This is an important beginning for the modern idea of an unconscious mind, but also revealed the nature of his atomic monads, which only have the minimal awareness needed to act and to react. It is probably better if we do not speak of monads as minds, because Leibniz is demonstrating that nature can only be explained if it has a minimal active power of initiative, and a minimal passive power of responsiveness. He attributed to each monad a 'living force' (which is the earliest expression of the modern concept of 'energy'). He went further, and said that each monad must contain the laws of nature, which requires each monad to contain a map of reality, and the role played by the monad.

When he was 30, Leibniz spent a week discussing philosophy with Spinoza in The Hague. The result was great mutual respect, and profound disagreement. They concurred on the existence of God, but Leibniz was shocked by Spinoza's pantheism (which identified Nature with God). Leibniz accepted most of the standard arguments in favour of God's existence, meaning that God must exist, as a separate spiritual, omnipotent, wise and perfect being. He also rejected Spinoza's monist view of the mind (as a single substance with physical and mental aspects), and accepted the dualist account of Descartes. He later offered the claim that if the physical brain were expanded to a vast size, and someone could walk around inside it, all they would see would be mechanisms, like the inside of a water mill, but no one could ever see the mind, which must therefore be a spiritual entity.

He was then faced with the interaction problem, which requires any dualist theory to explain how such different things can affect one another. A solution being discussed at the time was Occasionalism, which said that God continually co-ordinates the actions of mind and brain, so they appear unified, even though they are separate. Leibniz rejected this, because God's creation could never require such continual intervention, and his own theory (known as Parallelism) is that God creates mind and body to run in perfect synchronization, but without contact. He compared this to two perfect clocks, which are started in the same position, and so always tell the time identically.

The main aim of empiricists is usually to understand contingent truths (the way the world *happens* to be), whereas rationalists focus on the necessary truths (how reality *has* to be). Extreme empiricists say there are no necessary truths, and extreme rationalists usually say that all truths are necessary. Similarly, because empiricists favour experience, they are suspicious of a priori knowledge (the grasping of truths purely by thinking about them), whereas rationalists are optimistic about pure thought, which can give insights into reality. Leibniz was a rationalist. He had great confidence in the power of reason, believing that every necessary truth can (in principle) be proved, and that the basics of geometry and language are innate (born within us). He based his entire system on two principles: the principle of Sufficient Reason says there is a reason for everything, and the principle of Non-Contradiction says conflicting statements can never both be true.

The need for self-evident principles was his main criticism of empiricism. He wrote that empiricists expect the sunrise from habit, but the wiser astronomers expect it from reason. The biggest problem for empiricists is that evidence will not reveal necessary truths, and yet we clearly know many facts (such as mathematics) which just have to be true. For Leibniz necessities are always known a priori (only thought can show what must be true), and also the revelations of a priori thought are always necessary (pure thought always shows what must be true). This close connection between pure thought and necessary truths is a hallmark of rationalism, but has since been challenged in many ways.

Leibniz was the first person to ask the huge question 'Why does something exist, rather than nothing?', and he also offered an answer, involving his famous account of divine creation. God has to exist, and the arguments imply that God is perfect, so Leibniz investigates what follows from this. Being perfect, God knows all possibilities, and also how all things can be consistent (by eliminating contradictions). Hence prior to the Creation, God understands all the 'possible worlds' (an important new concept from Leibniz), each of them an internally consistent set of monads. Leibniz said there is a possible world where a hunting dog could smell its prey a thousand miles away. Something has to exist to fulfil the nature of all these possibilities, and the Creation was God's selection of the best world from among them.

The best world has the greatest quantity of reality, and this is found in the world which combines the greatest variety with the greatest order. Hence the world we live in is (in a famous phrase) the 'best of all possible worlds'. The immediate puzzle with that is why there are so many terrible things in our world, some produced by nature and some produced by humanity, and Leibniz wrote at length on the subject. His final answer is simple – that there has to be a trade-off. A possible world in which there are no natural or human evils would be greatly diminished, and nowhere near the rich reality of God's preferred world. To be reconciled to evil, we must see the whole picture.

A consequence of the idea that the best possible world must contain maximum variety is Leibniz's belief that no two objects are ever identical. They can only be identical if everything true of one is still true if we substitute the other one, which (he said) can never be the case for two objects. He once spent an enjoyable afternoon challenging Hanoverian courtiers to find two identical leaves in a garden, which they were unable to do. His principle known as Leibniz's Law says that if two objects are identical (that is, they are one object) then they must have identical properties. His Law is often cited in modern discussions, such as whether the mind is identical to the brain.

Leibniz had no interest in the extreme scepticism which Descartes tried to solve (such as that we are deluding ourselves about the world, or some other force is deluding us). He thought that our ability to predict future events shows most clearly that the commonsense view of reality is correct, and he even criticized excessive doubters for trying to invent doubts about what is obviously true. He did not, however, accept the commonsense view of the world as a set of visible objects, since there is no significant difference between a wall and a pile of bricks, and he did not believe (as platonists might) that properties and universals exist, other than in our language and thought.

He is also notable for seeing that relations may be needed in a full account of the world, but he denied that they have a distinct existence. The ratio between the lengths of two lines, for example, isn't a property of either one of the lines on its own, so it can't be located, so it can't exist. Space and time are also not real entities, but mere aspects of the relationships that arise from the ingredients of the world. Leibniz conducted a famous correspondence with Samuel Clarke, an English follower of Isaac Newton, in which Leibniz defended the relative view of space against the Newtonian view that space is a real entity. The idea that the universe could be moved sideways, or advanced a minute into the future, is absurd, he said. In general, reality is the hidden structure of monads, but the way we divide reality is just conventional, and done for human convenience.

Leibniz can be seen as the high point in the system-building approach of rationalist philosophy, just as John Locke probably constructed the best system for scientific empiricists. But each approach contains problems, which only emerge when a great thinker explores the issues. The place of the mind in a physical world is a persistent problem. Descartes and Berkeley showed that we cannot take the external world for granted; once we think carefully about physical objects, it becomes hard to see what unifies them. New difficulties began to appear about the nature and reliability of concepts and language. The authority of science was beginning to rival the traditional status of philosophy. Progress had been made with politics, but ethics and logic were still largely unexplored, other than by the Greeks. These challenges now had to be faced.

CHAPTER 8

LIMITS OF PHILOSOPHY (1739–95)

The Scottish philosopher David Hume (1711–76) began his greatest work, *A Treatise of Human Nature*, at the age of 23. The philosophers he admired were the empiricists Hobbes, Locke and Berkeley, and most recent empiricists consider Hume to have given the best statement of their position, because he was much more cautious than his predecessors. He rejected rationalism, seeing mathematics as a mere tool for thought, and he was persuaded by Locke that innate ideas (upon which rationalists rely) were non-existent or unknowable. He agreed with Berkeley that we have no concept of generalized eternal triangles, because we can only visualize one particular triangle at a time. He also rejected extreme scepticism about reality, and saw that if you are totally sceptical then you eventually doubt your own reason, which makes philosophy impossible.

He called his own preferred starting point 'mitigated scepticism', meaning that all beliefs must be supported by clear evidence. His first step was to explain the relationship between our experiences and the ideas we have about them. His view was that every single idea in our minds arises either directly from an experience, or can be tracked back to experience as its starting point. As an example he explained the fairy tale idea of a 'golden mountain' as having to originate by combining the two experiences of seeing gold and seeing a mountain. All of our ideas, he said, have a similar basis.

Above: Hume started from experience, but emphasized the limitations of reason, and of our ability to understand ourselves and the world.

He divided ideas into two groups – those that arise directly from an experience, called 'impressions', and those that result from relating impressions together, which are the 'ideas'. This gives us two types of knowledge – matters of fact, and relations of ideas. Science is matters of fact, and logic and mathematics are relations of ideas. This led him to a dramatic and influential conclusion. If we hold beliefs which are neither matters of empirical fact, nor relations of ideas with an empirical foundation, then they are nonsense. In a famous phrase, he said that books containing such empty beliefs should be 'committed to the flames'.

Locke treated the mind as a *tabula rasa*, on which experience writes our knowledge. Hume saw that this is a bad theory, because if a mind is completely empty then it cannot do anything with experiences. He offered his theory of Associations to explain how the mind turns experiences into knowledge. A mind, he said, does not have inbuilt ideas, but it does contain fairly automatic ways in which ideas are linked together, once they have been formed by experience. His three principles of association are Resemblance, Contiguity and Causation. Resemblance is instantly seeing that two things are very alike, as when a portrait suggests the person portrayed. Contiguity (closeness) is when a place conjures up something connected to it, such as your home and its neighbourhood, or we connect two simultaneous events. Causation is the jump we make from an effect to its cause, such as an artefact suggesting its maker. The three principles of Association are the unthinking connections between our ideas. At a more conscious level, we can deliberately connect ideas by reasoning, or by imagination (as with the golden mountain).

His theory of knowledge left no room for traditional metaphysics. He took an object to be unified by the way we think of it, rather by having something like a 'substance' or an 'essence' which binds it together. If a ruined church is rebuilt, for example, we happily accept it as the same church, and forget about the break in its existence. An object is just a bundle of impressions, and we can talk about it in any way we please. He also agreed with Berkeley that we cannot distinguish the objective primary qualities of an object (such as shape) from the more subjective secondary qualities (such as taste).

He didn't accept that objects have powers, or potentiality, or probabilities, because these are just memories of past patterns of behaviour, and cannot be directly observed. We can only assess possibilities by imagining what might happen. Like most empiricists, Hume thought there was little to say about necessary truths (which must be true), because no experience could show us what must happen, or what could never happen. The first humans, for example, could not have predicted that fire will burn us, or water drown us, and in another world the laws of nature might be quite different.

Hume shared Locke's pessimism about the future of science, because we can never get beyond the limited range of human experience (even with the help of instruments). He criticized the two styles of reasoning on which science is based – asserting links between cause and effect, and inductive reasoning, from a series of observations to a general conclusion. His problem with causation is that we normally say that an effect *has* to occur when the conditions are right (as when paper must ignite at a certain temperature), so that there is a necessary connection between cause and effect. But there is no empirical evidence for this supposed necessity, and for all we know any routine cause might suddenly produce a surprising effect. All we see is the regularity of one type of event (high temperature) followed by another (flames), and the necessity of the outcome is just a strong feeling of expectation, which can only be explained as a habit, and not as a fact. Causation, he said, is merely a 'constant conjunction' between events, which we can think of either as a pattern we have noticed, or a strong feeling of anticipation.

He made similar comments about induction. If we all observe that daffodils are yellow over a long period of time, we eventually agree that 'daffodils are yellow'. Newton said that science relies on this principle, because a law is just a generalization about nature, with no exceptions. Hume demanded to know what observations support such a huge claim, given that we only ever observe a tiny proportion of these supposed universal truths. Induction implies that repeated observations gradually increase our certainty, but Hume asked why we would be more certain after a thousand observations, if we weren't certain the first time. Induction seems to rely on the assumption that the future will be like the past, but what observations could ever prove *that*? His explanation of inductive truths was the same as his explanation of cause and effect – that general truths are just based on habit. His account of the laws of nature is now known as the 'regularity' theory.

Hume had little to say about the relationship between body and mind, presumably because no evidence threw any light on it. He did, however, have views on Locke's new concept of a 'person'. The nature of a human being is fairly obvious, but what experiences can reveal the essential person, or self, or ego? Hume searched inside his own mind, and all he could find was a 'bundle' of continually shifting experiences and ideas. Even Locke's reliance on memory to unite a person over time doesn't work, because the impressions involved continually change. Hume concluded that we just imagine that we have a self. As we might expect, Hume also rejected the idea that we have free will, because we cannot tell where our choices come from.

The dream of the Age of Reason was to give a rational justification and explanation for all human beliefs, but thinkers were slow to address the problem of morality. By 1700 the work of Spinoza was almost unknown, and most thinkers (especially those with religious commitments) were unhappy with the best-known proposal, which was the view of Hobbes that morality is just a strategy by selfish people to benefit themselves by making contracts with other self-seeking people. Critics of this view defended the idea that we have a natural moral faculty (seen as 'conscience' or 'intuition' or the 'moral sense'), and the main debate concerned whether this faculty relies on emotion or on reason.

Hume's main view on morality was summed up in a famous paragraph. He observed that moral writers often say what 'is' the case, and then move on to what 'ought' to be the case, but Hume could never find any reasoning that leads from one to the other. That is, our supposed moral duties are never proved by any facts or evidence. This is now known as Hume's 'is-ought' distinction, and (more generally) it raised the question of whether values have any basis in facts. Hume concluded that morality is not a matter of reason, and dramatically summarized his view by saying that someone who was willing to see the whole world destroyed just to avoid having their finger scratched might seem very strange, but they are not actually irrational. Morality may not be rational, but neither is it a clever way to be selfish, because people are not entirely selfish by nature. Hume concluded that morality arises from our natural feelings of sympathy for one another. We wince when others are in pain, and Hume said even unpleasant people don't tread on the foot of a person suffering from gout, so we all have some concern for others which is not totally selfish.

The next question is why morality should prefer these friendly feelings to self-interest, and the answer lies in the social benefits we gain from kindness. This brings his theory closer to that of Hobbes, because the aim of morality is benefit, but Hume saw the aim in social rather than individual terms. We collectively prefer a society where we help one another, and the traditional virtues are guidelines for how these benefits can be achieved. One of the main benefits we all seek is security, so Hobbes was right that we need a strong social authority, though it may not be an absolute monarch.

Hume expressed doubts about the social contract theory (that only the will of the people can bestow authority). The idea that society rests on an agreement struck him as an idle daydream, because we are simply born into a society, and have little choice but to accept it. Telling people that political power needs everybody's agreement is just asking for trouble. Locke's idea of 'tacit assent' – that the mere use of social facilities implies agreeing to them – also struck Hume as empty. He agreed that we are all naturally equal, but that was of little use in politics, because if you restored everyone to their natural equality they would quickly become unequal again. He also rejected Locke's claim that property is the foundation of social justice and order, because everyone knows that most property was originally acquired in an unjust way.

Like Hobbes, Hume was an atheist, and after his death his discussion of the arguments for God's existence were published. He rejected the ontological argument (that the mere concept of God implies existence) on the grounds that nothing has to exist, and the claim 'God does not exist' doesn't seem to be a contradiction. He rejected the cosmological argument (that existence needs a starting point) because if we can say that the First Cause must exist, why can't we just say that all the other causes must exist?

The main problem with the teleological or design argument (the favourite of most believers) is that it relies on analogy. We say orderly nature implies a designer because an intricate instrument like a watch implies a designer, and we know that watches do have designers; so nature must also have a Designer. The problem is that application of the analogy must be consistent. Faults in the watch imply a bad designer, who may be incompetent or inexperienced. A huge complicated machine implies several designers. Most good designs result from trial and error; some orderly patterns, such as those among numbers, arise with no designer at all. Hume also rejected miracles, on the grounds that when faced with the normal laws of nature, miracles are so unlikely that they should always be treated as lies or misunderstandings. Medieval theologians had criticized some of the arguments for God's existence, but it was a new development for a philosopher to challenge all of them.

Hume drew negative conclusions from his mitigated scepticism in almost every area of philosophy. We believe in many of the things he rejected because of habitual common sense, which Hume was happy to accept, but it is impossible to prove any of them. Reason is seriously overrated, and Hume described it as 'the slave of the passions'. Ancient scepticism had suggested that we can't believe anything at all; Hume's scepticism said that in order to live we must accept all sorts of normal beliefs, but that we can never be sure of any of them.

IMMANUEL KANT (1724–1804)

Kant was a quiet, middle-aged and obscure philosophy professor in the German city of Königsberg, on the Baltic Sea coast, when his world was shaken by an encounter with the philosophy of David Hume. This caused him to start his philosophy all over again, and within a few years he published his *Critique of Pure Reason*, one of the great books in the history of the subject. Kant was provoked into asking new questions, aimed not just at the traditional topics of philosophy but also about the very nature of rational thought.

What impressed him was Hume's suggestion that some of the grander claims of metaphysics might actually be meaningless, because they had lost touch with experience. Kant started out in the rationalist tradition, and greatly admired Leibniz, but he could see that this empiricist challenge was right. So Kant's new question was not about *what* we know, but *how* we know.

Kant thought that Hume's theory of Associations was a serious over-simplification. Far from being a *tabula rasa*, the mind has a complex mechanism for receiving and making sense of the incoming impressions, and Kant set out to assess this mechanism. His first step was to clarify Hume's concept of an impression, which Kant called an 'intuition'. An impression is raw uninterpreted data, such as a patch of red, or a brief sound, but our actual experience might be of tomatoes or music, so Kant's main claim was that concepts and categories are involved in every experience, and without that nothing counts as an intuition.

He called his main tool for identifying these concepts and categories a 'transcendental argument', which works backwards from some fact or experience to what must be presupposed by it (as in 'I am walking, so I must have legs'). After careful analysis he proposed that there are four basic groups of category, which are Quantity (such as size), Quality (such as soft), Relation (such as inside), and Modality (such as possibility). He then claimed that these categories are necessary (they could be no other way), and that they don't just shape our experience; but that experience is impossible without them. Since the categories are necessarily this way, there is only one possible conceptual scheme, shared by all rational beings.

Above: Kant tried to unravel the way we experience things, showing why thought is limited, and knowledge depends on the nature of our minds.

Kant agreed with Leibniz that necessary truths (which must be true) can only be known a priori (by pure thought), and that anything known a priori is necessarily true. But the challenge of David Hume warned that a priori thought has limited scope, because it doesn't involve experience. One agreed form of a priori knowledge was of analytic truths, which are true because the predicate is contained within the subject, such as 'a child is a young human', in which 'young human' is part of the concept 'child'. We can see that such a sentence is true without experience of children. Kant's transcendental arguments work backwards into our conceptual scheme, by analysing our analytic concepts until we arrive at the basic ones that cannot be analysed further. Hence a priori knowledge is possible, provided it only concerns our own thoughts.

Kant's next big question was 'Is a priori synthetic knowledge possible?' That is, can pure thought extend our knowledge, rather than just analysing it? He offered examples that seem to qualify. 7 + 5 = 12 is said to be synthetic, because the concept '12' is a new one, not contained in '7 + 5'. That two straight lines cannot enclose a space, or that only one line through a given point can be drawn parallel to a line, are truths about space which are necessary, and known a priori, but also extend our understanding of space. Kant defended this claim against empiricists, because he said such knowledge anticipates all possible experience, and so doesn't depend on experience.

Having cautiously defended the power of pure thought to extend our knowledge, Kant was then firm about its limits, and said over-confidence about a priori synthetic knowledge is like a dove wishing it could fly in outer space. The most famous claim for a priori synthetic knowledge was the Ontological Argument for God's existence (used by Anselm and Descartes), which was rejected by Kant because no concept, not even 'God', is extended by containing the concept of 'exist'. You learn nothing new (and synthetic) about a concept when you learn that the item exists, because only experience can teach us of existence. Hence a priori thought can reveal the necessities of our conceptual scheme, but its most important power was to show the limits of our thinking. A major topic in all philosophy after Kant is marking the apparent limits of our knowledge, but also looking for ways to extend it.

Despite his respect for empiricist restraint, reason has the leading role in Kant's philosophy. He rejected strong scepticism about the external world, because he thought that would be 'the euthanasia of reason', and it seems obvious that scepticism about mathematical knowledge is absurd. However, as Descartes had shown, reason needs a reasoner, so Kant needed a role for the Self, despite David Hume's doubts about our ability to ever experience such a thing. A transcendental argument shows that there must exist a person who unites the trains of thought found in reasoning. So we must be committed to a unified Self, despite having no experience of it. The same reasoning led Kant to a commitment to the existence of free will, which he saw as part of the essential nature of pure reason, even though Spinoza and others had shown that the causes of our acts of will are hidden from us. Kant remained neutral about the relationship between mind and body, since no a priori thought can reveal which theory is needed to explain our experiences.

Kant was committed to experience, and to the mental equipment (of a free self and a conceptual scheme) which is essential to make experience possible. These things can be known a priori, and are therefore necessarily true, and can be known with certainty. But what of the external world? He weighed up Locke's distinction between primary qualities (which reveal facts) and secondary qualities (which are much more subjective), but had to reject the distinction, because nothing in his conceptual scheme could explain it. His conceptual scheme included traditional concepts such as 'substance' (unified entities) in order to explain change, but these are a priori concepts and not observed facts. More surprisingly, he concluded that both space and time have a similar a priori status. That is, we see the world through space-time spectacles, and have no way of experiencing space and time as separate realities. Hence the basic fact that substances endure through time is part of our thinking, rather than an observed feature of reality.

At this point Kant's philosophical system is drifting into the idealism of Berkeley, but Kant was not willing to go that far. Strictly speaking, his thinking implies that reality is unknowable, and we are trapped in our ideas, but Kant felt that only an external reality could explain experience. He therefore distinguished between the 'phenomena', which we experience, and the 'noumena', which are the true facts of reality that trigger our intuitions or impressions. Kant is committed to the existence of this unknowable noumenon, and talks of the 'thing-in-itself' of an object, in addition to its experienced qualities. However, Kant's comments on this waver between realism and idealism, and the next generation split into two camps over the existence of the thing-in-itself.

Kant's great book tried to show the limitations of reason and knowledge, but his very rational theory of morality is a high point in the optimistic Age of Reason. In the spirit of the Stoics, Kant took the aim of humanity to be living rationally, but how could this be achieved? The consequences of our actions can be very unpredictable, so the rationality has to be in the intentions, and rational intentions must concern principles. Every thoughtful action involves, he said, a 'maxim', which is a simple statement of the principle which is being followed (as when closing your front door aims at the rule 'keep my home secure'). The hallmark of rational behaviour is consistency and avoidance of contradiction, so right actions must aim at consistency in the maxims. Since the target is rationality, this target is not personal but universal consistency (like correct answers in mathematics), so we must ask 'What maxim should *everyone* follow in this situation?'

He thus arrived at his famous Categorical Imperative (that is, the undisputed command of morality), which says 'So act that the maxim of your action can be willed as a universal law.' The simplest version of this asks 'What if everybody did that?' It means, for example, that it is morally wrong to drop litter, because we cannot want a society in which people constantly drop litter. His examples of immorality are actions which imply a contradiction, such as breaking a promise, which can only be done if we believe that all promises should be broken – and no one thinks that. When deciding on an action, we should find a maxim which we think everyone should follow, and it is then our duty (as rational beings) to obey that maxim. The only motivation for this is the existence of a good will, which is the basic requirement of morality.

People aim at their own happiness, which is fulfilling their own desires, but the aim of universalizing the principles we follow is to respect everybody's aims, and not just our own. Our own happiness is unimportant. As Kant memorably put it, the aim of doing our duty is not to be happy, but to be 'worthy of happiness'. Having rejected the standard arguments for God's existence, his account of morality added the necessity that the distribution of happiness according to worthiness must be a real possibility, so we must believe in God (the just power), eternity (the time for justice) and an afterlife (the place of justice). This is Kant's Moral Argument for God's existence.

We must respect the desires of other people because they are rational. Kant depicted as an ideal the Kingdom of Ends, in which all rational minds meet as equals, and every contribution is weighed according to its truth. For Kant this excluded animals from moral life, but it did imply respect for any contributor, no matter what their age or social or educational status, and this had obvious political implications. The ideal of Liberal Democracy was emerging, and was supported by Kant. He endorsed the democratic idea of the social contract, which Rousseau had made famous, because each rational individual has equal importance, and good laws need open criticism. Kant identified exploitation as one of the great evils, because that uses people as a means to some end which is not their own. War, he said, could only be justified if it has been agreed by the soldiers who have to fight, and that hardly ever occurs. His consequent desire for peace as a great social ideal led him to add an international aspect to the social contract, because it is no good having rational agreement within each state if the states then fight like wild animals. The idea of international law emerged from Kant's political thinking.

Kant remains famous for his rational accounts of moral duty and liberal politics, but his most important influence is in obliging philosophers to think about what we now call their 'conceptual scheme'. His commitment to the ideals of the eighteenth-century Enlightenment is shown in his belief that all rational beings have the same concepts and categories for thought, which implies that rational people can reach a consensus in his Kingdom of Ends. Many later thinkers rejected this optimism, saying that there are innumerable conceptual schemes, arising from local cultures, historical and economic situations, religious beliefs and assumptions based on gender.

CHAPTER 9

POLITICS AND IDEALISM (1750–1861)

The French Revolution of 1789 was so dramatic that it influenced the whole intellectual life of Europe, as well as its politics. The possibility that the structure of society could be changed was also a great stimulus to philosophy. The philosopher who had the greatest influence on the Revolution was Jean-Jacques Rousseau (1712–78). He is best known for his book *The Social Contract* (1762), but his influential thinking was not confined to politics. Hobbes saw the natural life of humans as very brutal, and needing authority to make it pleasant. Rousseau disagreed, and offered a revolutionary view of human nature.

The brutality, he said, was caused by the early formation into competitive tribes. Prior to that people existed in small groups, lived directly off the land, had no need for violence or theft, and were impossible to organize or discipline. They were happy because they were too busy to become envious or bored, and suicide was almost unknown. Society deprived us of this state of

Above: Rousseau took an optimistic view of humanity, but wanted to give people control over the excesses of the state.

freedom and equality, and is the cause of our unhappiness, rather than its solution. As he memorably expressed it, 'Man is born free, and he is everywhere in chains.'

Not only did life become harsher when societies were formed, but it also became more rational, which led to a decline in morality, because reason suppresses our natural feelings, making us more selfish. True morality, he said, should be guided by a combination of self-interest and the sympathy we show when we cry while watching a play. Rousseau became famous for praising delicate and lofty feelings (known as 'the sublime') rather than reason and science, and what started as a fashion for enjoying beautiful landscapes gradually grew into the Romantic movement that emerged after 1789.

His aim in politics was to regain the equality and freedom which humanity once enjoyed. In the modern world freedom is not living in the wild, but living by social laws which are agreed by everyone. He liked the idea of a social contract, but saw the obvious problem that the original agreement occurred long before the citizens were born, and might now be corrupted. Hence he proposed an assembly of all qualified citizens (in his view, adult males who worked), which would meet regularly and be the ultimate source of power. The aim of the assembly would be to reach an agreement which would be as nearly unanimous as possible (known as the General Will), not about actual government decisions, but about the way the state would be governed. Constitutional laws would be passed which delegated power to a ruling group, who in turn would appoint leaders. The leaders would then have power over the people, but they could be recalled if they were corrupt, and the citizens would be happy to obey the laws which they had helped to create.

Rousseau understood that it is difficult to know the General Will, because of the problems with any democracy. It is vital that citizens vote for the national interest, rather than their own, and they must not be influenced by coercion or fashion, so he disliked political parties, and wanted minimal discussion before a major vote. The assembly of the people has supreme power, but Rousseau was not a democrat in the modern sense. Regular elections of the actual rulers leads to continuous bitter disputes, each new group of rulers reverses the decisions of the previous group, and between elections the losers are effectively slaves. He rejected hereditary monarchs and aristocrats as actual rulers, because they are untrained and often foolish, but elected aristocrats might be possible. A referendum is particularly bad, because it undermines the authority of the governing group who were appointed by the people.

Although Rousseau's ideas stirred revolutionary feelings in France, he felt that revolutions are best avoided, because the enthusiasm for freedom becomes excessive, and a return to slavery is the usual result. A state religion is essential, but Christianity will not do, because it undermines loyalty to the state, so Rousseau designed his own minimal state religion, which he felt would be acceptable to all denominations, who should then tolerate one another.

JEREMY BENTHAM (1748–1832) AND JOHN STUART MILL (1806–73)

During the Enlightenment, moral thinking moved from virtues of character to the quest for simple rules of correct behaviour which could be used in a law court to judge the morality of an action, rather than the person who performed it. The idea that good actions should follow moral intuition or conscience seemed right, but how could these be assessed or agreed upon? Kant offered a universal rule which he derived from pure reason. Jeremy Bentham became famous for proposing the theory of Utilitarianism, which was much simpler. Good actions, he said, are those which produce happiness, and bad actions are those which cause suffering. The motives and predictions before an action are of no moral importance; all that matters are the consequences, which are easy to observe and assess. We might even assign scores to possible outcomes, and then calculate our moral actions.

Morality concerns pleasure and pain because these two govern our whole lives. All that matters about the pleasure and pain is their intensity and their duration. Hence what causes the pleasure is unimportant, and it doesn't matter who experiences it. A simple game can be more valuable than great art, and the delight of a pauper matters more than the mild pleasure of a monarch. Such a simple claim has led to many criticisms, the most important of which is that all other values are neglected as long as the desired end is achieved. It seems that we can lie or break promises, and distribute the goods of society very unfairly, as long as pleasure is maximized and pain avoided. Despite such problems, Utilitarianism has many attractions, since making people happy seems an obviously good thing to do.

The influence of Utilitarianism on politics has been enormous. There is no elitism about Bentham's moral aims, and not only are all human beings equal in their entitlement to pleasures, but animals also qualify, according to their capacity for feeling. Institutions that fight for animal rights arose directly from this new theory. It is no coincidence that the anti-slavery movement also began to grow, and a landmark publication was Mary Wollstonecraft's 1792 book *A Vindication of the Rights of Woman*, which urged that women are equals who are only held back because their educational opportunities are restricted. Although Utilitarianism does not guarantee a fair distribution of benefits, it gives priority to people who are suffering. Modern government departments have to be very utilitarian, and it is hard to imagine a better way for hospitals to make difficult decisions.

Above: Jeremy Bentham wanted a moral system as precise as the law, and based it on the pleasant and unpleasant consequences of each action.

John Stuart Mill was the son of Bentham's great friend James Mill, and his book *Utilitarianism* of 1861 is the most famous work on the subject. His main change to Bentham's simple theory was to propose that quality of pleasure matters as much as quantity, summed up in his remark 'Better to be Socrates dissatisfied than a fool satisfied'. Mill also summed up the political theory of democratic liberalism, which had emerged during the Enlightenment, in his book *On Liberty* of 1859. This offered a highly individualistic view of society and promoted freedom as the highest value, because that would maximize benefits for most people, as Utilitarianism requires. His essential social principle was that people should be entirely free in their lives, apart from the restraints needed to prevent them interfering with the freedom of others. This gave political importance to the influential idea that each person has a 'private life', in which their behaviour has no effect on other people, and should therefore be totally free. A further implication was that government interference in even the public lives of

Above: Mill thought quality of pleasure mattered more than quantity, and he defended liberal freedom in politics.

citizens should be kept to a minimum. Mill agreed with Spinoza and Kant that freedom of thought and speech must be given particularly high priority, because progress is stunted without it.

GERMAN IDEALISM (1795–1830)

After the excitement of the French Revolution, and Kant's major rethink of how we relate to the world, Germany became the centre of creative philosophy, with the university town of Jena as its focus. Although Kant promoted the possibility of freedom, because each individual controls both the way they see reality and their own moral choices, some worries began to emerge about conflicts within his system.

Friedrich Jacobi, a conservative Christian who preferred faith to pure reason, saw problems with Kant's commitment to the thing-in-itself (as what causes our experiences). For Kant, causation is not a feature of the world, but one of his 'categories of the understanding' located in the mind, so Jacobi said there is no external relation to things-in-themselves, and therefore no reason to believe in them. This means that Kant is an idealist (with no belief in external reality), even though he tried to deny it. Since this idealism seemed incompatible with religious belief, Jacobi labelled the resulting view as 'nihilism' (not believing anything).

Kant had a further problem, because he viewed experience as a two-stage process, in which the mind passively receives 'intuitions' (raw sensations), and then very actively turns them into experiences by interpretation. If we then ask 'What is consciousness?', it is both passive and active, which seem to be incompatible. Karl Reinhold rushed to Kant's defence, and said that consciousness consists entirely of 'representations', which stand between the self and the external world of things-in-themselves. Hence Kant is both consistent, and not an idealist. Further critics pointed out, however, that pain doesn't involve representations, and that Reinhold implies that the self is just representations of representations. So Kant was back in trouble, and philosophy was felt to be in crisis, faced with nihilism, or Humean scepticism, or some form of idealism.

An immediate line of escape was seen in the ideas of Spinoza, which suddenly became popular. If Kant's theory contained conflicts, Spinoza offered a united theory in his pantheist single substance, combining nature, mind and God. This was controversial, because it might imply atheism, but it suggested that we need a general view of nature, as well as a general view of the mind's experiences. So the challenge for young philosophers was to produce a theory which would give an account of the self, its interpretations, and the natural world, which would fit into a united system and imply modern views of morality and politics. Johann Fichte (1762–1814) arrived in Jena with just such a theory, which offered idealism as the solution.

With Fichte we meet a great increase in the obscurity of written philosophy. Kant's new terminology demanded hard work from his readers, but with Fichte we move to another level. Clear summaries of such thinking are not only difficult, but are sometimes seen as a betrayal of ideas that are very subtle. Immersing oneself in the original texts may be the only route to proper understanding.

In his *Science of Knowledge* of 1794 Fichte started from the most minimal supposition possible, which is (following the Cogito argument of Descartes) the existence of the self, as whatever is raising the problem of its own existence. He went further than Descartes, though, because the self is not only a rational being, but must also (following the arguments of Kant) be understood as free, and as 'spontaneous' (making a creative contribution to its own experiences). He took free will to be obvious, and was amazed that Spinoza couldn't see that in his own daily life. Since the essence of the self is the ability to freely generate its own rules, the self is not a thing, but a source of activity.

The next step is Fichte's most original idea. For the self to be able to make free rational judgements, it must be able to both assert and deny things. But denial needs the concept of negation, to think of what is *not* the case, as well as what *is* the case. Since his starting point is the self, there must be an immediate grasp of whatever is not-self, which sets limits to the self, and is the world about which we are thinking. This means

Above: Fichte saw the free creativity of the self as the basis of thought, an idea which founded the German idealist movement.

that our understanding of the world is based within ourselves, which implies idealism. This is confirmed when he says that the distinction between subjective and objective truths must itself be subjective – which means that our entire understanding is subjective. Hence Fichte denies the existence of things-in-themselves, and a judgement is seeing relationships between concepts, not assessing external evidence.

In Fichte's account the self is very creative, and posits what is needed for understanding. This includes one's own body, since freedom implies the possibility of action. Idealism always threatens to become solipsism (all that exists is my own mind), but we must also posit the existence of other minds, which help to produce the limits to our own thinking. There is a religious dimension to Fichte's view, because the essence of a mind is a 'striving', which is to grasp everything, including God. There is no place for external nature, but his theory seemed inspiring because it was unified, and emphasized dynamic individualism.

The 1790s saw the emergence of the Romantic Movement in literature, which led to an emphasis on feeling rather than classical reason and order, and resulted in exciting new achievements in the arts. The origin of the movement, however, was mainly philosophical. Three figures stand out: Friedrich von Hardenberg (a poet, known as 'Novalis', who died in 1801 at the age of 28), Friedrich Schlegel (1772–1829, a critic), and Friedrich Schelling (1775–1854). They were impressed by the active 'spontaneity' of the mind seen in Kant, and the emphasis on freedom in Fichte, but felt that something was missing, because Fichte's view of the self is too theoretical, and his denial of the thing-in-itself cuts us off from nature.

Novalis was interested in the possibilities and limitations of philosophy. A complete system should make us feel 'at home' in the world, and so it must include nature, as well as an idealist view of the self. Nature, however, is vast, chaotic and constantly changing, so a clear and complete system may be a nice ideal, but it is beyond us. Novalis wanted to either grasp nature as a whole or to get closer to its details, rather than to produce theoretical systems. The best thing philosophy has to offer is problems, and to those the expressive language of poetry or the unfolding stories in novels may be the best response.

Novalis was an idealist, but his creative ideas are extended to include nature. Mind and world are not, though, seen as separate, but are a unified whole (as Spinoza suggested), and the soul unites the two worlds, especially through the creations of art. Our self-consciousness must be seen as an aspect of something much greater. The human

Above: The Romantic poet and philosopher Novalis emphasized how we are part of nature, which must be included in any idealist system of philosophy.

body is not just 'posited' but is actively involved in thinking, and pure sense experience is important.

Friedrich Schlegel agreed that rational systems are inadequate, mainly because nature is a process, whereas systems are static. Although the unification of mind and nature is what we hope for, there is a gap, but the gap can be bridged by imaginative poetic creations. What matters to Schlegel is not just poetry and philosophy, but also the attitude we adopt to the world, and for romantics this should be ironic. This is not just playing with words, but showing an awareness of our limitations. We yearn for order when faced with disorder, we yearn for infinite love but are merely finite and human, we are passionately committed but coolly detached – and our ironic attitude to the world should match these conflicts.

Friedrich Schelling looked for a way to unite the active self with nature, and found it in productivity and freedom. Nature is endlessly creative, and so freedom is its very essence, and the creativity of all human beings (not just artists) shows the self as an aspect of nature, just as idealism has shown that nature is an aspect of the self. He used the term 'the Absolute' to name this union, which is an idealist version of Spinoza's single substance. The Absolute is a totality of the ideal and the real, which goes beyond the distinction between subjectivity and objectivity, and beyond disputes about the thing-in-itself. To understand the Absolute became the aim of idealist philosophy, and it acquired a religious (and often mystical) aspect.

Schelling focused more on nature than previous idealists had done. He saw nature as Becoming (rather than static Being), so that processes of increasing self-awareness are its essence (an idea which implied evolution). He saw nature as having three stages: matter produced by forces (an idea drawn from Leibniz), light, and living organisms (the highest level). This organic view rejected the picture of nature as atoms controlled by laws, and influenced scientists as well as philosophers. The huge emphasis by Schelling on freedom, both in nature and in the self, became an important theme for future philosophers.

GEORG HEGEL (1770-1831)

Hegel, who was greatly influenced by Schelling, created perhaps the most complete philosophical system, and achieved great fame as Professor at the University of Berlin. Ever since Descartes had been sure that he had a mind, but not so sure that he had a body, there had been a gulf between nature and our idea of nature. Hobbes solved that by saying the mind is physical, and idealists solved it by saying that nature is ideas. Hegel belongs among the idealists, but he wanted a unified picture.

He rejected the romantic idea that nature is a chaos which can only be understood through works of art. Hegel preferred the stoic picture of nature as profoundly rational. However, he made a distinction between Reason, which is the essence of nature, and human understanding, which is severely limited. Most importantly, human understanding, unlike nature, is gripped by contradictions, built into our concepts, which it is the task of philosophers to clarify. He took a historical view of how our scheme of concepts progresses through a series of tensions and conflicts, moving towards an ideal clarification which coincides with the Reason in nature. This is the progress of Spirit, which is the collective awareness of humanity. The ideal is to understand the Absolute, which is the combination of nature and the fully rational system of concepts which express it, and the end to which idealist historical thought progresses. Art is merely a historical stage in the development of Spirit (though Hegel shifted the main focus of aesthetics from beautiful landscapes, which are uninteresting, to human works of art).

Above: Hegel's great system emphasized our confrontation with creative contradictions, and the role of history in our developing understanding.

Conventional understanding gets stuck when our concepts contradict one another, and logic forbids further progress. Kant, for example, observed that we cannot possibly have free will, and yet we must assume we have free will. Hegel evaded this problem by using Fichte's idea that the idea of the Self immediately implies the concept of the non-Self. All concepts have the feature of immediately implying their own negation, because the concept can only be understood by seeing the contrast. Hegel saw this as a tool for developing a system of ideas. Instead of traditional dialectical argument, by giving reasons and counter-reasons (which always hits the brick wall of contradictions), Hegel saw philosophy as observing the unfolding of the implications of concepts, because the negation of a concept produces a new concept (with its own further negation). Truth is the authenticity of a concept, and of its network of implications, which leads to the Absolute – a structure of perfect rational coherence.

The ideal of a philosophical system is to start with minimal assumptions (such as the Ego of Descartes, or the Impressions of Hume), but Hegel spotted a way to start with no assumptions at all, by beginning with the concept 'nothing'. That is a little more than nothing, because it is the concept of nothing, and concepts have negations. 'Nothing' can only be understood in contrast to 'being', and starting with 'being' would imply 'nothing', so this pair is the foundation of idealist thought. If we focus on the transition from nothing to being, a third concept emerges, of 'becoming'. This process of thought is Hegel's revised concept of 'dialectic', which arises from concepts rather than reasons. Hegel's book *The Science of Logic*, completed in 1816, tracks a long sequence of concepts built by the dialectical process, which gain in precision and breadth as they progress, and lead to a large group of conceptual categories, which control our thinking in the way outlined by Kant.

Kant thought there was only one correct conceptual scheme, but for Hegel the categories are appropriate for a particular culture at a particular historical moment. Because the Spirit of each age is a step in the progress towards a grasp of the Absolute, Hegel remains an optimist about the validity of the categories he identifies; they just await improvement. He is an idealist, so our reality is this structure of thought, but there is no real gap between ideas and reality, because our concepts converge on a wholly rational ultimate truth. As an idealist he denies the thing-in-itself, but he is not cut off from some unreachable reality, because our concepts and nature form a unity, and Spirit is the self-awareness of nature. Hegel was a committed Christian, and saw a rational grasp of the Absolute as something like union with God. Orthodox theologians did not take to his system, but Hegel saw himself as the champion of religion in an age plagued with doubts.

The implications of Hegel's very abstract metaphysics have been highly influential. The Enlightenment had seen rational thought as the short cut to a universal consensus about what is true, but Hegel's emphasis on history and cultural variety undermined this view. The dream of rational consensus is just the ideal culmination of history, and not something we can expect here and now. In his system the influence of these changing cultures ran deep, so that we not only categorize experiences in this variable way, but human understanding is itself quite local in character, and (a particularly influential view) the character of each individual person depends on the culture they find themselves in. He criticized Kant's categorical imperative rule for morality, because it took no account of the cultural background.

Hegel emphasized Spirit to make us think of ourselves collectively, and freedom is a social concept, not an individual one. Man is not 'born free', but achieves freedom through the social institutions of the family, normal civil society, and the state. These create rights which bestow freedoms, but all freedoms must be asserted by individuals (so that even slaves only have a right to freedom if they claim it). No one can be fully free in a society, because even if you can choose whatever you like, the available options are created by other people. Hegel didn't accept the social contract theory (because you must already have a society to make contracts). He also disliked democracy, because it led to the oppression of the minority, and because elected representatives have narrow interests. The best hope was an enlightened state which values freedoms and sees the larger view. Since the history of Spirit is a progress towards freedom, he was optimistic about this.

KARL MARX (1818-83)

Despite the thoroughness of Hegel's political theory, the next generation was sharply divided over how to interpret it. Conservatives liked the need for state authority, and revolutionaries liked the emphasis on historical progress. In the early 1840s the Young Hegelians took the revolutionary line, led by Ludwig Feuerbach (1804-72) and Karl Marx. Feuerbach accepted many aspects of Hegel's philosophy, but he felt that the emphasis should be on conscious sensations rather than on concepts, and he rejected Hegel's religious view of the Absolute. Feuerbach was an atheist, but he aimed to explain why people believe in religion; the concept of God must be seen in entirely human terms, as simply an idealized image of what humans would like to be. Feuerbach's highest ideals were justice, love and wisdom, and these are attributed to the God of Christianity.

Marx too wanted to explain religion without accepting it, and he saw reality in entirely physical terms, despite his acceptance of Hegel's historically developing conceptual scheme. Marx was very struck by the accelerating industrial revolution, and his dramatically original idea was to see human concepts and categories as changing responses to economics and social power, rather than to Hegel's rational progress of Spirit. Instead of a dialectical development of concepts, history is the emergence of one class from another. Typically, one powerful class, such as warlords, or landowners, or wealthy capitalists, bring into existence an opposition, and people identify closely with their class because there is class warfare. Only a revolution can break out of this.

Much of Marx's discussion concerns the modern middle class (the 'bourgeoisie'), who block progress towards true freedom. The bourgeoisie like liberalism, which gives them the right to create their own freedom, for which they have sufficient wealth. Private property is a bourgeois device for excluding the workers (the 'proletariat'), and conventional morality, religion and the education system are bourgeois creations which pressurize the proletariat into subjection. The ultimate source of social values is control of the means of production in industry. The key idea is that social power not only controls lives, but also controls minds. Liberalism offers attractive ideas such as 'fair wages' and 'equal rights', but these turn out to be a 'false consciousness' created as a means of control. Marx's aim is freedom, but it must be genuine, and this is only possible under communism, in which people have full control of their own society.

No philosopher can equal the influence Marx had on subsequent historical events, but his account of the forces which control our thinking remains highly influential in philosophy. Kant said we had a fixed conceptual scheme, and Hegel said our concepts

Above: Marx saw the contradictions of Hegel's
system in practical economic terms, and
explained history in terms of class conflicts.

evolve, but Marx said the way we see the world is at the mercy of social forces. He retained Hegel's optimism about progress, but since Marx it is much easier to see that 'eternal' truths are moulded and changed by the people around us.

CHAPTER 10

MAVERICKS (1819–1910)

After Hegel became a professor at the University of Berlin in 1818 he was the dominant figure in European philosophy, and most students mastered his new vocabulary and embraced some form of his idealism. The main philosophers of the next generation, however, were individualists and rebels. Arthur Schopenhauer (1788–1860) was infuriated by the obscurity and lack of explanation in the lectures of first Fichte and then Hegel. He particularly disliked Fichte's rejection of Kant's thing-in-itself, and preferred Kant's 'transcendental' idealism. He hated Hegel's commitment to the Absolute and to the importance of the state, and scandalized the university by arranging his own lectures to coincide with Hegel's. However, the students remained loyal to Hegel, and Schopenhauer lectured to an almost empty hall.

His earliest writing was about the Principle of Sufficient Reason, which he saw as a tool from which a system could be built. Since there is a reason for everything, we can dispense with presupposed categories of thought and concepts of experience, because we can infer them from reason, or derive them from perception.

Schopenhauer proposed four modes of explanation: we explain objects by their causes, concepts by their grounds, mathematics by the nature of space and time, and ethics by studying motive. Although enquiry is the exploration of the reasons for things, Schopenhauer rejected the stoic view that nature itself is entirely rational, and said that some things are inexplicable.

The two great limits of our understanding are our ignorance of the Self, and of the actual thing-in-itself (which robust realists accept). What we can know are our experiences of representations, and the activity of our own will, with our sense of reality arising from these. This thought led to Schopenhauer's great work of 1819, *The World as Will and Representation*. He took the will to be not merely a theoretical entity which might possess 'freedom' (which he doubted), but the most important aspect of our minds (as opposed to reason, which was the usual candidate for that role).

Strictly speaking Schopenhauer is an idealist, because he took reality to be the focal actions of the will, and the

Above: Schopenhauer rebelled against the vagueness of much idealism, and built his views on the ways we explain things, starting from the human will.

will is part of the mind, which is definitely not physical. But by seeking the network of causes among experience, we can reach out towards the thing-in-itself, and build a successful picture of what we accept as reality. The activity of the will gives us a direct experience of such causation, and its control over the body links us to what we represent as external. In this sense, Schopenhauer said that the will *is* the thing-in-itself, because it is the most real thing we know. In his view the conscious mind is entirely a combination of willing and representing, because consciousness does not exist apart from these roles. Our intellectual aspect is found in these activities, because we constantly derive concepts, causes and reasons to cope with our experience.

Most thinkers (other than Hume) had seen the Self as the guiding force of a mind, but Schopenhauer noted that the word 'I' is ambiguous, meaning both the passive entity which knows and the active entity which wills. The active will is the only aspect of the Self we can know, and that seems to change continuously. The will itself is driven by a combination of character and motive, and to explain those he placed great emphasis on the unconscious mind. Most of our acts of will are explained by desires, fears and reasoning which are hidden from us. Our main unconscious motivations are selfishness and malice, but also compassion, which he valued highly.

Our inability to control our own thought and motivation makes the will a source of misery for human beings. Schopenhauer is famed for his pessimistic view of life. Life, he said, has no purpose, apart from the satisfaction of desires, and the will's drive to satisfy unending desires is what makes us unhappy. This becomes obvious to us when we are bored, and on the whole we would all be better off dead. The prospect of rebirth is horrifying, and most of us would commit suicide if the act were made swift and easy.

As consolation, Schopenhauer offered the pleasures of knowledge and (above all) of works of art. He wrote extensively about aesthetics, and saw art as freeing us from our imprisonment in the relentless desires of the will. Unlike the romantics, he saw art as more concerned with ideas than with feelings. Like Kant, he found in art an experience of the world that was 'disinterested', and offered an insight into a less personal mode of reality, which he identified with the world of Plato's Forms.

He took ethics to be based on our natural feeling of compassion. He thought Kant's rational approach to morality was hopeless, because behaviour can be thoroughly nasty even when it is rational. In neither art nor morality is rational theory much help when it comes to practice. The other problem is that the only other motivation we have (apart from compassion) is self-interest, and that is the precise opposite of morality. He saw morality as a very individual affair, and had little interest in politics, seeing defence as the main role of the state.

Schopenhauer was an atheist, and particularly disliked the Christian idea that the world is evil. However, he applauded the social role of religions in encouraging uneducated people to take life seriously. Because he saw the Self as obscure and continually changing, and because compassion is the one true virtue, he became attracted to Buddhism later in life. He admired the way Buddhists start with the vices (lust, laziness, anger, greed and hatred), and only once these are understood should we aspire to the virtues (which are pity, justice, courtesy, wisdom and honesty).

Schopenhauer was neglected until late in life, but he ended his days as an admired (if rather daunting) public figure.

SØREN KIERKEGAARD (1813–55)

Having studied theology at the University of Copenhagen, Kierkegaard read Hegel and attended Schelling's lectures in Berlin. Like Schopenhauer, he hated this German idealism and rebelled against Hegel's historical view of human lives, which only find their significance within a wider community. All of the systematic philosophers seemed to miss the point, because their systems were more like timeless mathematics than like guides to living. Even Socrates (Kierkegaard's hero), who had turned the attention of philosophers to morality, only discussed moral knowledge, but never discussed the daily reality of ethical living.

Kierkegaard returned home to Denmark and began a series of books (many written under pseudonyms) designed to challenge conventional thought. Like Socrates, he became a familiar sight on the city streets, and said his aim was to 'create difficulties' for his readers. His main aim was to lead them away from abstract theorizing, and to seek the right attitude to the business of living. In traditional terminology, he moved the focus away from Being to Becoming. He wasn't interested in classical scepticism, and he took the reality of the human situation in a concrete world for granted.

He abandoned the idea of truth as objective correctness, because he found language to be full of bias, and reason just relied on finding contradictions, which he mostly found amusing rather than revealing. He therefore treated truth as a mental state, which cannot involve certainty, but involves authenticity, faith, honesty and passionate commitment. This is truth in the spirit of 'she is true to herself', or 'he is a true hero', rather than 'this is a fact'. What matters is striving to attain a state of truth which can be a beacon to guide a life, and it needs to be endlessly affirmed and repeated to achieve this result.

Above: For Kierkegaard, what matters is not grand theories but our individual lives, to which only authentic commitment can give meaning.

Kierkegaard saw passion and commitment (rather than reason) as the essence of life, which echoed the spirit of Romanticism. There are three modes of commitment: the aesthetic life (the normal life, centred on pleasure); the ethical life (searching for duty); and the religious life. Kierkegaard was a Christian, and had studied theology. To reveal the distinction between the ethical and religious lives he examined the story of Abraham and Isaac in the Book of Genesis, in which God commands Abraham to sacrifice his only son. Abraham sets out to obey, and would have committed what appears to be a deeply immoral action, but God intervened. The text praises Abraham for thus demonstrating his fear of God, and Kierkegaard agreed. The highest form of life involves the 'teleological suspension of the ethical' (done for some higher purpose), and this takes us into the world of faith.

He did not think God's existence can be proved, but his Christian belief remained unshaken, and he pioneered the modern concept of faith in God as a subjective commitment, rather than an objective assessment of the facts. His most famous image sees faith as a 'leap'. This is often seen as a leap over an obstacle, or as a great leap into the unknown, but what Kierkegaard had in mind was a dancer's leap, which soars into an unknown realm, but then returns to reality, equipped with a new perspective.

Kierkegaard remains most famous for his account of the ethical life, which embodies what we now call Existentialism. He did not believe in a fixed Self, but saw it as a synthesis of pairs of opposites, which are senses of the finite and infinite, of the temporal and eternal, and of freedom and necessity. The Self seeks change for its own sake, so we must struggle to achieve authenticity, which is 'striving to become what one already is'. The most vivid part of this is confronting complete freedom of choice, which he called a 'yawning abyss'. This results in a state of 'anxiety', which may not be a bad thing. We have to train ourselves to be anxious in the right way. If we succeed, our ethical choices are good not just by doing the right thing, but by doing it with an energetic and intense commitment. Although we understand life with hindsight, he said, it can only be lived by moving forwards.

FRIEDRICH NIETZSCHE (1844–1900)

Nietzsche was the son of a German pastor and a brilliant young classical scholar, but he soon abandoned his Christianity (by

Above: Nietzsche wanted to enhance individual human lives, by seeking healthy values to channel the unconscious drives that dominate us.

'instinct', he said), and he was too unorthodox to pursue an academic career. He eventually settled for a solitary life in Switzerland, and in the 1880s produced a sequence of unconventional and challenging books. His hero was Schopenhauer, but he had no sympathy with his pessimism. Nietzsche also had no interest in the idealism of the previous generation, was a realist about the physical world, and accepted Darwin's new account of evolution as natural selection. The great challenge in this wholly physical world was how to reject nihilism, which was the apparent loss of all values that threatened us when religion declined and objective science took over.

For Aristotle philosophy began in wonder and perplexity, but Nietzsche said it begins with horror and absurdity. His main aim in philosophy is the 'ranking of values', and he built a picture of life that would help us to do that. However, he saw philosophizing as a very personal affair, and expected thinkers to live according to their beliefs. He was little interested in logic and 'pure' reason, and said philosophical thought is more like wrestling or dancing.

His view of thought in the ancient world was strikingly unorthodox. He admired the traditional virtues of honour, decisiveness and integrity seen in the epic poems of Homer. When Socrates introduced the democratic idea of dialectic (which gives authority to reason, rather than to people), Nietzsche felt that this undermined the traditional values which had united Greek society. Plato seemed even worse to Nietzsche, by introducing an idealistic belief in Forms which had nothing to do with real life, and thus destroying the values which had made Greek culture supreme. Christianity produced the final collapse in the system of values, by turning their ranking upside down. The values that marked out a good slave, such as humility, concern for others and conformist obedience, became the highest values for a good Christian, and the values of the great aristocrats which Nietzsche admired, such as pride, self-esteem and military courage, were now seen as wicked. Christianity also preferred faith to thought, and branded many of the pursuits of a normal healthy life as evil.

Nietzsche was a realist about the external world, but cautious about the concept of truth. The big problem is that we over-simplify the world. For example, proofs succeed in formal logic because precise and unwavering values are assigned to the symbols and letters. But reality is never precise and unwavering, so the logic is disconnected from reality. It is the same with mathematics, scientific laws, and any activity that tries to use precise concepts or categories. Instead, we just have individual people with their own 'perspectives' on things, and the best we can hope for is a picture built up by combining our perspectives.

Nietzsche was not a complete relativist (like Protagoras, who denied truth), but was greatly struck by the varied viewpoints of different cultures. For him, the important question was not to define the nature of truth, but to ask why truth is seen as important. In ages dominated by mythology or great communal passions the quest for precise truth seems irrelevant, and the desperation to know the truth is often a sign that something has gone wrong. For Nietzsche what matters is not truth or knowledge (which may be unattainable) but our beliefs, because it is beliefs which guide how we live. Since scientific objectivity seems almost impossible, he saw no sharp distinction between values and facts.

Nietzsche admired Schopenhauer's reliance on the will and our experiences. He did not share the dualist view of the mind, however, and so the will is basic to the whole of nature, and not just to people. He called it the 'will to power', and it is not only seen in human actions but also in the conflict we observe if we drop two chemicals into a test tube. This force is experienced in humans as what he called 'drives', and almost everything significant about a person can be explained by a shifting pattern of dominant and subservient drives, which are sometimes well co-ordinated and sometimes fragmentary. The Self is just a fiction, and the only thing which truly unites these drives is the body which contains them. The drives are largely unconscious (and a bit frightening), and Nietzsche dismissed consciousness as a very superficial aspect of life.

One of his books was called *Beyond Good and Evil* (1886), which expressed his frustration with the conventional morality of his age. Societies become stuck in rigid systems of values which survive from earlier times, and are thus unable to create the fresh and living values which are needed for the best sort of life. Nietzsche's quest was for new forms of life which might be possible, if only we could free ourselves from authoritarian and rigid convention. He dismissed all of the standard theories of morality. Ancient virtue theory relies too much on a fixed view of human nature, and is therefore too conservative and conformist. Kant's categorical imperative aimed for moral laws which are universal, but morality should be entirely personal, and Kant's theory makes obedience the highest virtue. Morality can't be based on contracts, because those are only made between equals, and people are not equal. He was particularly scornful of Utilitarianism, which absurdly aims for universal 'happiness', which is boring, and cripples the possibilities of human development.

Nietzsche also denied free will, since we obviously don't control what we think. Because our drives are largely unconscious we cannot even know our own intentions or motives, never mind the consequences of what we do. We are left with 'instinct' as the guide to action, and we must generate healthy values to inspire our instincts. The values of which he approved include honesty, bravery, politeness, insight, sympathy, and solitude. He considered hope to be a vice. Since our drives are the only motivation we have for action, they are mostly self-interested, but that is not a bad thing, because even love can be understood as a form of self-interest.

Nietzsche is an early existentialist thinker, because he sees morality as an assertion of authentic individual values. Like Kierkegaard, he was more interested in Becoming than in Being, but he differs from later existentialists in his denial of free will, and in the very limited ability we have to change our own nature. He too saw boredom as a positive quality, because it reveals a yearning to be active and creative.

Among more democratic thinkers, Nietzsche is notorious for his elitism. The sign of the 'higher type' of person is that their drives are more unified and focused than in other people, so they have clear individual goals, and are more successful in achieving them. This makes them superior, but he often uses the word 'healthy' to distinguish these admirable people from highly focused criminals. After his death the Nazis admired Nietzsche, and he certainly approved of the qualities of independence and determination which they showed, but Nietzsche despised racism, and would certainly have seen the Nazis (who later included his own sister)

as 'sick' rather than healthy. The most famous extreme case of the higher type is the Übermensch (the 'Overman'). These rare individuals, who include artists and teachers as well as military leaders, show complete independence in the creation of values, which inspires the rest of us, who can do no more than follow.

Like Schopenhauer, Nietzsche placed a high value on art (and especially music). In his early works he saw art as the highest ideal of life, but in his later thought it was merely an expression of what is most valuable. He frequently praised dancing (and apparently danced himself, when alone). He liked the idea that a life could in itself be a work of art. He found especially illuminating the idea of Eternal Recurrence – that we might have to live exactly the same life over and over again. On the one hand, if life is meaningless, then it is a sort of victory to confront this nihilism forever, and on the other hand we can try to pursue a life which would be worthy of such endless repetition.

Nietzsche was not a great political theorist, but his love of many elitist and aristocratic values led him to despise democracy as an attempt by the weak to restrain the strong. He thought the social contract was an absurd idea, since most societies are the result of conquest and power. He did, however, think that citizens should participate in their society, but only if their aim is to improve it. Some of Nietzsche's views may sound alarming, but he was a charming man and much liked by those who knew him. His career came to a sad and premature end in 1889, when he suffered a complete mental collapse. The cause is unknown, but he spent his last few years in the care of his sister – a fate he would not have welcomed.

CHARLES SANDERS PEIRCE (1845–1910)

While the philosophers were contemplating idealism, social revolution and individual authenticity, the scientists had been making remarkable progress. New planets were discovered, the surface of the Earth was mapped, the mechanism of evolution was revealed, heat and energy were understood, and electricity was brought under control. Above all, the nature of matter was revealed as composed of many elements, which culminated in the discovery of the structure of the Periodic Table.

Auguste Comte (1798–1857) pioneered the idea that the philosophy of the future should be guided by science, rather than by abstract speculation. He saw the history of civilization as dominated first by theology, then by metaphysics, and finally by Positivism, which was his idea that all knowledge is scientific, and is always based on observable evidence. There are limitations to what can be known, but Comte had high hopes that science would not only reveal great truths, but would also solve our major social problems. Metaphysics would disappear, because science gradually reveals all the broad general truths, as well as the solid details of observation. Positivism had many followers, and this attitude to science remains very influential.

Charles Sanders Peirce (pronounced 'purse') was the first major philosopher from the USA, and he too saw philosophy from the point of view of the sciences. This attitude made him very cautious about metaphysics (which he dismissed at one stage as 'moonshine'), but he developed an account of general ideas based on the methods of experimental research. He saw metaphysics as a completion of the scientific picture by extending it into a clarification of the obvious common sense behind science, and into the realm of what is possible, rather than actual. He said the reasoning in metaphysics is quite simple – but the concepts involved are extremely difficult.

In an age when German idealism was still popular, Peirce aimed for precision and analysis. He was one of the first modern philosophers to say that logic is a necessary tool for exact thought. He pioneered the detailed account of different types of relations between things, and he introduced the distinction between type concepts and token concepts (so that if I say 'no! no! no!' I have spoken one word – the type – and three words – the tokens). He was the first to notice the interest of 'indexical' words,

Above: Peirce founded American Pragmatism, which took science as basic, and saw knowledge in terms of successful practical predictions.

such as 'now' or 'here' or 'we', which depend for their meaning on the situation in which they are spoken. Peirce said the role of indexical words is to make us more observant, by drawing attention to our immediate situation. He became interested in the general theme of signs and symbols to represent ideas, and began what is now the science of semiotics. He identified three families of signs: icons represent what they resemble, an index is a natural sign, and a symbol is conventional. His aim was to understand our categories of thinking by studying the language in which we express them.

Peirce understood the force of idealist and sceptical arguments against realism, and agreed that doubt about reality is possible. His own view, though, was that we must hope that realism is true and objective facts exist, because otherwise science is a waste of time. He viewed logic as rooted in reality, and said that we get our concept of a contradiction from experience, not from pure ideas.

His concept of truth was unusual, and based on his optimism about science. He totally rejected the idea that science has discovered any certainties, or is likely to, but we must nevertheless accept successful science as our best knowledge. He thus introduced the idea of Fallibilism into the theory of knowledge – that (contrary to Descartes) we can know things without being certain of them. He defined truth as the ultimate knowledge on which the sciences slowly converge. Truth is thus the aim of enquiry, rather than its achievement.

Inductive reasoning (generalizing from examples) is basic to scientific thought, but Peirce recognized the difficulties involved. A multitude of similar observations can never make a future exception impossible. But for Peirce there is more to it, and we need the wider picture. If chemists, for example, have pure and standard ingredients, they don't need to keep repeating an experiment. Induction only gives a strategy if you have many observations, but what if you only have one, and what are we to make of the first observation in a series? For this, said Peirce, we need creative imagination, to picture possible explanations (a procedure he called 'abduction'). This influential idea has led to modern accounts of science based on explanation, rather than on logical deduction.

Peirce is most famous as the chief founder of the American Pragmatist school of philosophy. As a reaction to idealism and sceptical empiricism, the aim was to get back to the real world, where human understanding looks to the future, and asks of each proposal 'does it work?' (rather than 'do we know it?'). For Peirce, it was a theory about how we should think of things. Rather than view objects as substances with properties, he said our whole conception of an object consists of the possible effects it might have. A concept is defined as the possible experimental outcomes it could lead to. A belief is not a mere mental state but a rule for action (which makes beliefs more important than knowledge or truth). Ethics should not concern general theories, but the immediate possibilities of what can be done. In general, the Pragmatism of Peirce is a theory for settling meanings, and especially of key terms in science.

By the beginning of the twentieth century Pragmatism was acquiring many followers, especially when it was popularized by William James (1842–1910). James was primarily a psychologist, and introduced the idea of a pragmatic theory of truth, an idea rejected by Peirce. This roughly says that something is true if it is useful, making truth the hallmark of successful action. Modern thought in the USA is greatly influenced by Pragmatism, which is seen as typical of American culture.

CHAPTER 11

ANALYSIS (1879–1951)

The division between Analytic philosophy, mainly practised in English-speaking countries, and so-called 'Continental' philosophy, mainly practised in Germany and then France, is said to have begun with the dispute in the 1790s over how to interpret Kant. The division became much clearer after 1900, with the introduction of phenomenology by Edmund Husserl in Germany, and Bertrand Russell's writings on mathematics in England.

A modern Analytic philosopher must understand Propositional Logic, Predicate Calculus, Set Theory and Modal Logic. The technically minded will add Intuitionist Logic, Formal Mereology, Many-Valued and Paraconsistent Logics, and maybe even Category Theory. The precise methods of analysis which result from such techniques have produced a style of thought which can now be found in ethics, political theory, philosophy of language, metaphysics, philosophy of mind, epistemology, applied ethics, feminism, and even aesthetics. Here is a brief outline of the main technicalities.

Propositional Logic was developed by the ancient Stoics, but given precision by George Boole (1815–64). His big idea was to use the symbols of algebra to map the relationships between thoughts. It concerns the relationships between complete sentences (or 'propositions', the unambiguous ideas behind sentences), which are linked together by the 'connectives', which are *and* (.), *not* (¬), *or* (v), and *if-then* (→). The propositions can then be linked by the connectives to form complex statements. Thus the sentence 'if he did this and no one helped him then he's either crazy or a genius' could be symbolized as (D.¬H) → (CvG). Sentences can then be proved or disproved using the rules of use for each connective.

Predicate Calculus was created by Gottlob Frege in 1879, to define the logic used by mathematicians. He introduced letters for variable items (x, y, x), letters for specific objects (a, b, c . . .), letters for predicates or properties (F, G, H . . .), and two quantifiers (∃, ∀) to say whether a sentence refers to some or all of the items. The four standard connectives are still used to link sentences, and proofs remain the same. The sentence ∀x∃y(Fy.Gy) says 'for all the xs there is a y which is both F and G' (such as 'there is always at least one student who is both clever and difficult').

Set Theory was developed by a series of people, most notably Ernst Zermelo (1871–1953). It is the logic of grouping objects. It uses Predicate Calculus, with a new symbol – Ɛ – which means 'is a member of' (or 'is in'). So for 'Zermelo is German' we can write a Ɛ G, meaning he is a member of the set of Germans. The set G consists of {g1, g2, g3 . . . }, which lists all the Germans. The reasoning is based on a set of carefully devised axioms, such as 'if two sets have the same members they are the same set', and there is an empty set (written '{ }').

Modal Logic was devised by the American C. I. Lewis (1883–1964) to give a logic for what is possible or necessary. It simply added two symbols to Predicate Calculus. The symbol □, called 'box', represents 'necessarily', and ◊, called 'diamond', represents 'possibly'. If I said 'He may have to go home', this is understood as 'it is possibly necessary that he go home', and symbolized as ◊□Ga. In modern versions the logic is interpreted in terms of 'possible worlds'. So ¬◊∃x(Cx.Sx) says no x can be both C and S (so 'no possible world contains circular squares').

GOTTLOB FREGE (1848–1925)

Frege, a professor at the University of Jena, was the founder of Analytic philosophy. His first book created Predicate Calculus, but his *Foundations of Arithmetic* of 1884 was more philosophical. He aimed to give a precise account of the essential nature of numbers. He rejected psychology or experience, and tried to show that numbers are based in pure logic. Of particular importance was his strategy of identifying true sentences about numbers, and then infer-

Above: Frege created modern logic, which he saw as revealing a rational world, if we eliminated the ambiguities of ordinary language.

ring what exists from what those sentences refer to. He concluded that numbers exist as abstract 'objects'. With Frege, language
(rather than knowledge) became the central issue of philosophy,
because it reveals how we understand the world much more precisely and reliably than Kant's project of trying to explain how
we think.

The most puzzling feature of language is the nature of meaning.
Frege's contribution was to see that meaning has at least two
components. He pondered the case of the discovery in the ancient
world that the bright star seen near the horizon in the morning
('Phosphorus') is the same body as the star seen near the horizon
in the evening ('Hesperus'). The puzzle is that the identity of
Phosphorus with Hesperus was a great astronomical discovery, and
yet the information it contains is trivial – that an object in the sky
is identical with itself. Frege said the meanings involved have two
components, a description with a 'sense', and the picking out of the
object, the 'reference'. The fact that the names refer to one thing
makes it trivial, but discovering that two different descriptions
refer to the same thing can be a revelation (like 'the man in the blue
suit is the murderer'). Frege created two branches in the philosophy
of language, the study of sense or pure meaning, and the study of
reference (the connection between words and the world).

Frege not only created Predicate Calculus, he also asserted a new
importance for logic in philosophy. He inherited the stoic idea
that nature itself is rational. This rationality is not embodied in
the physical world, which is vague and imprecise, but in what he
called the 'third realm' of existence (the other two being mind and
body). Hence he viewed our exploration of the network of logical
implications as a revelation of the abstract heart of reality, and

many modern Analytic philosophers see the study of logic as a way to study metaphysics.

Frege's main project is known as Logicism, the theory that arithmetic is essentially a form of logic. Arithmetic had been shown by Giuseppe Peano to rest on a small number of simple axioms (basic assumptions), and a logicist must show how these axioms can be derived from pure logic. Frege's next big book set out to do this, but it relied on the principle that every concept has an extension. The extension of the concept 'cow' is the complete set of actual cows, past, present and future. If every concept has such an extension, then Frege could derive the numbers from logical concepts. In a famous letter, Bertrand Russell proved to Frege that it is impossible for every concept to have an extension. This undermined Frege's great enterprise, and since then support for the logicist idea has dwindled. However, Frege's work was very little read until Russell drew attention to it, and praised his achievements. Since then Frege has deserved his status as the founder of a major school of thought.

BERTRAND RUSSELL (1872–1970)

If Frege originated Analytic philosophy, then Bertrand Russell firmly established it. He aimed to use the tools of logic, Set Theory and verbal analysis to give precise foundations for mathematics, knowledge, language and science. He had limited interest in aesthetics, political theory and ethics (though he wrote extensively on political issues, and believed that ethics should be understood through politics). He wrote with exceptional clarity (by the standards of philosophy), and aimed to support every proposal with valid reasons and well-chosen examples.

Russell pursued Frege's Logicism project to reduce arithmetic to logic, even though Russell had identified major problems with Frege's work. Russell tried using the newly emerging tool of Set Theory to define the foundations of arithmetic, and joined the struggle to find the best axioms for the job. Although his complicated system had some success, critics have said that Set Theory makes too many assumptions to count as pure logic. In the course of this work Russell explored ways in which natural languages such as English can be fitted into the precise framework of logic. Frege had given us the concept of the 'reference' of a word, but there were puzzling cases. If true sentences refer successfully to things, what do false sentences refer to? The claim 'unicorns don't exist' doesn't seem to refer to anything.

Above: Russell saw logic as the key to all of philosophy, and focused the new Analytic School on the ideal of precision and clarity.

Russell developed the revealing idea that a sentence in English has a 'logical form' hidden beneath the surface, and precise logic can show what was really meant. He famously took a puzzling sentence ('the present King of France is bald', which seems to be meaningful but doesn't refer to anything, because France no longer has a king), and said that while it appears to be talking about some entity, a concealed part of the logical form makes a claim that this person exists. Since the King doesn't exist, the sentence is false (rather than meaningless). This theory of Definite Description was very influential, because Analytic philosophers began to examine many confusing sentences, and clarified them by expressing them in formal logic. Since then, the main use of logic among philosophers is not to prove things, but to express ideas with maximum precision.

Over a long career Russell shifted his opinions on almost every major issue. He gradually abandoned belief in any sort of fixed Self, and came to think that mind and brain involve one substance rather than two. For a long time he believed in the existence of sense-data – that is, there exist mental states which are produced by experience, and which are in turn interpreted by the mind. The point was that you could then discuss knowledge in terms of interpreted sense-data, while leaving the question of how the sense-data connect to reality as a separate issue. He gave up sense-data because they don't actually explain anything; if perception relies on sense-data then that means we need sense-data in order to perceive sense-data.

Russell had a strongly realist view of reality. When the cat disappears behind the furniture, it is absurd to say it briefly ceases to exist, and there must be facts about the distant past which can never be observed or known. He defended the correspondence theory of truth, which says a sentence or a belief is true if its content 'corresponds' with the external facts. Russell tried to map out the way the ingredients of a sentence can match up with these facts. He proposed that relations must be a real feature of the world, because parts of what we say must correspond to them (as in 'Edinburgh *is north of* London').

He saw our picture of the world as a combination of sense-data and logical inferences, a theory he called Logical Atomism. Thus physical objects are composed by us from lines, shapes and colours, and the existence of the object is the conclusion of a swift and hidden deduction. From these minimal beginnings we can go on to deduce laws of nature and great general truths, thus completing Frege's vision of mapping the logic of reality. Subsequent thinkers have attempted to extend this daunting project.

LUDWIG WITTGENSTEIN (1889–1951)

Wittgenstein came to England from Vienna to study aeronautics, but soon became a pupil of Bertrand Russell at Cambridge. Intense and charismatic, he greatly influenced his teacher; his *Tractatus Logico-Philosophicus* of 1921 explored issues raised by Russell.

He followed the empirical tradition of David Hume, which asserted that anything which was not either science or 'relations of ideas' such as logic should be dismissed as meaningless. Wittgenstein concentrated on the nature of logic and of meaning in language. Russell believed that the rule-based connectives (*and, or, not,* and *if-then*) exist as abstract objects, in an eternal non-physical mode of reality, but he had doubts, and asked Wittgenstein to investigate. The pupil concluded that his teacher was wrong, and said the logical connectives are simply rules which are true by definition. The word 'not' is just a rule for reversing the truth or falsehood of a sentence, like a verbal light switch. Hence all of logic is meaningful, but it is also trivial.

Wittgenstein followed Frege in believing that language shows the limits of our reality. His conclusion was that logic reveals nothing about reality, so that leaves only science, which is truths grounded in experience. This meant that even ethics is outside language, and nothing meaningful can be explicitly said about it. The remaining task for a philosopher is to explain *why* so much of the language of metaphysics says nothing at all, and that needs an explanation of meaning.

His strategy followed Russell's Logical Atomism. Modern logic is structured around objects with properties, so the 'elementary' propositions assert that a single object has a single property. Language is built from such atoms of language, so any complex statement can be analysed into these basics. If some components of a complex sentence are not reducible in this way, then that shows that they are meaningless. Using Frege's new concept of reference, Wittgenstein said that the foundation of meanings is individual names, which simply

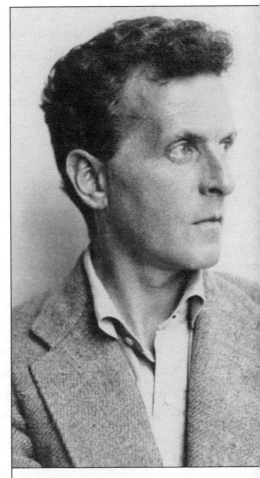

Above: Ludwig Wittgenstein deflated the big claims of logic and metaphysics, and shifted the focus to the way ordinary language is used.

mean the thing they pick out. Our account of existence rests on either names or variables (such as 'x') in a precise language.

Truth is understood as a successful match between an atomic proposition and a simple fact or 'state of affairs'. Wittgenstein explained the match with his 'picture' theory. The picture given by a sentence embraces a chunk of reality, and then the structure of the picture 'reaches out' to the structure of the fact. The meaning of normal sentences can then be understood in terms of truth. A sentence means the picture of reality we would have if the sentence were true (known as the 'truth-conditions' theory).

The second half of Wittgenstein's career is so different from the first that it looks like the work of a different thinker. He retired for several years, and then rejected the precise logical atomism of his own *Tractatus*. He kept the anti-metaphysical view that our only knowledge is either scientific or trivial, but developed a new strategy for showing why our ideas are so confused, centred on the study of ordinary natural language. He thought philosophers had been 'bewitched' by their own language, and are thus trapped, like a fly in a bottle.

His earlier view that the meaning of the logical connectives is just the rules for their usage grew into a general view of language. The idea that there are 'meanings', which consist of references to objects, and truth-conditions for sentences, was replaced by the idea that language is understood entirely through the way it is used. As long as we can use the words 'and' and 'not' correctly, we don't need to know the rules involved. Philosophers are obsessed with theories, but language works without them. Words are like chess pieces, which are defined by what we can do with them, and not by their intrinsic nature.

An example of Wittgenstein's new view is his account of universals (general terms such as 'horse' or 'green', that refer to many different individuals). Platonists treat them as real entities with an abstract mode of existence, and nominalists dismiss them as just words, to be used in any way we like. Wittgenstein said they should be understood like 'family resemblance', when the faces of an extended family are recognizably similar, but to varying degrees. His famous example was the word 'game', which cannot be defined because there are so many borderline cases, and there is nothing which all games have in common. He went on to talk about 'language games', which are whole areas of our talk which have a rough core of assumptions but no clear definition. Followers of this idea discuss religious, legal, fictional, sporting and diplomatic language games, among many others. Such talk is felt to make sense only if you are committed to that particular 'form of life'. This is the beginning of the 'holistic' view of language, which says that sentences cannot be understood in isolation, but only as a part of wide-ranging language use.

The most famous argument in his later work is the Private Language Argument. Language is only possible because we can follow grammatical rules, but the point of rules is that you have to submit to something you didn't invent. If you are asked to continue the sequence 6, 8, 10, 12, you may promptly say '14', but the real answer might be '24' if some quite different rule were involved. Nothing in the sequence itself settles what the rule is. In the case of language, Wittgenstein claimed that only a community of speakers can produce the necessary rules of grammar and usage – hence a language which is private to one person is logically impossible.

His argument is controversial, but its implication is that we must give up the very individualistic picture of thought and knowledge implied by Descartes and his Cogito argument. The whole idea of learning by the introspection of a private world of sense-data has to be given up, and minds cannot be understood in isolation. The language of wine-tasting illustrates his point; the subtle personal experiences can only be expressed if there is a language agreed among the experts.

LOGICAL POSITIVISM (1925–40)

Russell and Wittgenstein aimed to weed out the rubbish in philosophy, and bring precision to language, by finding tests for what is or is not genuinely meaningful. In 1920s Vienna a group of thinkers including Moritz Schlick, Otto Neurath and Rudolf Carnap welcomed the new empirical approach, and admired the scientific Positivism of Auguste Comte. The result was the Verification Principle, which said that meaningful statements are either tautologies (such as definitions), or there must be some way of verifying whether they are true. Knowledge is thus divided into two groups. One type – the tautologies – is a priori (known by thought), analytic (true because of meaning), and necessary (has to be true). The other type is empirical (known by evidence), synthetic (true because of reality), and contingent (only happens to be true). Mathematics and logic are of the first type, and the sciences are of the second.

The theory has tough implications for metaphysics, religion and morality, because they don't fit in either group. Only scientific forms of metaphysics are acceptable, and big metaphysical claims about what is necessary are reduced to dull talk of definitions.

The emphasis on experience makes realism about objects difficult, and the preferred view was Phenomenalism, which says that a physical object consists only of the actual and possible experiences it can produce. A priori arguments cannot prove anything about reality, so the Ontological Argument for God's existence is ruled as invalid. Other arguments for God must meet scientific standards of evidence.

Moral principles are either definitions (which means they contain no facts), or they require observations to prove them, which seems impossible. The usual result is the Expressivist view of ethics, which says that moral statements are just expressions of emotion, and calling something 'good' is no different from applauding it. The question of whether other people than oneself are really conscious (the 'other minds' problem) suddenly became a difficulty, because we continually say what other people are thinking, but this can't be verified.

The big challenge for the theory was to accurately state the Verification Principle. At first it was said that the verification must be 'conclusive', and that the method of verification *is* the meaning of the sentence. Since verification is rarely conclusive, and methods are varied and inconsistent, the test had to be weakened. We must now say that evidence is always relevant to what is claimed, or that it implies some observations. It is unclear who must make the observations, which might be by animals, or people who are long dead or yet unborn. The Principle came under increasing attacks, the worst of which were that the Principle seemed to fail its own test, and that you must know what something means *before* you can verify it. The wildest speculations don't actually seem meaningless, even when they can never be tested.

Strict Logical Positivism was defeated by its own yearning for precision, but it remained highly influential. A.J. Ayer popularized its more controversial claims in the English-speaking world, and it launched big debates about ethics and the language used to express religious ideas. An important product of the movement was Gilbert Ryle's *The Concept of Mind* of 1949, which used the tough empiricism of the logical positivists and of behaviourist psychology to attack the dualist theory of mind (which Ryle labelled the 'ghost in the machine' theory).

WILLARD QUINE (1910–2000)

Quine was an American who visited Europe, where he studied Russell and the logical positivists (especially Rudolf Carnap). He was an empiricist, and derived his view of reality in the true analytic style, from his view of logic. The first-order predicate logic of Frege says that only objects exist, with predicates to describe them. Quine rejected second-order logic, which implies that the properties also exist, because we can never be clear about whether one property is the same as another. He also rejected Modal Logic because he was unimpressed by the existence of necessities and possibilities. Quine said that whether something is necessary depends on how you describe it. Seven is necessarily smaller than eight, but the number of days in a week only happens to be smaller than eight.

Quine's view of reality reflected his 'taste for desert landscapes', so he followed Russell in trying to reduce what we must believe in to a minimum. Instead of just asserting what we believe in, we can deduce our beliefs from the theories we accept, and Russell had showed that we can 'paraphrase' language to simplify the beliefs. Ontology is derived from our best theories, which are scientific. Our 'ontological commitment' is to whatever must exist to make those theories true. In his early career Quine was a nominalist, and only believed in the objects of standard logic. We can specify properties as sets of objects, so that 'red' means the set of all objects to which we attach the word 'red'. Later on Quine had to modify his Nominalism, because mathematics is essential for scientific theories. Nearly all of mathematics can be expressed in Set Theory, so Quine accepted sets as well as objects. Commitment to sets is a bit more than mere commitment to the objects in the sets; for example, you must accept the empty set, which contains no objects.

Logical positivism relies on the idea that 'analytic' knowledge is merely verbal, while 'synthetic' knowledge, such as science, relies on experience. Quine decided that the sharp distinction between analytic and synthetic was invalid. The arguments supporting the distinction are circular, and examples could be swapped. The standard modern example of an analytic truth is 'bachelors are unmarried men', which is known by analysing 'bachelor', but if those people were picked out by some other means (a genetic trait, for example), then the fact that they are unmarried might be a discovery of social research. Quine said instead of a neat division of knowledge we have a 'web of belief', in which any part of the web can be adjusted to suit simplicity and convenience (which showed Quine's Pragmatist tendencies). Even logic, which seems both theoretical and secure, might be changed to suit science (perhaps when faced with the strange objects of quantum mechanics). His web of belief faces the 'tribunal of experience' as a whole, rather than one sentence at a time, and a strong meaning of 'true' only applies to this whole. There are no foundations for knowledge, and adjusting our belief systems is like repairing the ship during a long sea voyage.

Quine reinforced his doubts about meaning in language by considering 'radical' translation, from a completely unfamiliar language into English. If the word 'gavagai' is spoken in the other language while the speaker is looking at a rabbit, we mustn't presume that the translation is 'rabbit'. It could refer to parts or qualities or processes of the rabbit, and good translation only emerges with immersion in the alien culture, and can never be perfect. Similar problems arise for rival scientific theories. Thomas Kuhn followed this up in 1962 by giving a holistic view of scientific theories, implying that each one can only be understood from within the theory, and genuine comparison is impossible.

Because Quine only accepted something as existing if it could be precisely reidentified ('no entity without identity' was his slogan), he rejected what philosophers wrote about knowledge, since no belief can ever be precisely identified. Instead he proposed that scientists take over the study of knowledge, and a whole area of study called cognitive science has since emerged. The aim is not to find elusive 'justifications', but to track the way in which experience turns into firm beliefs. Quine saw the mind as no more than brain processes, and a physical object as merely some chunk of space-time, so he is a model for anyone seeking the most minimal ontology possible.

CHAPTER 12

CONTINENTAL PHILOSOPHY (1900–84)

Analytic philosophers aimed to give an essentially scientific account of reality, using techniques from mathematics and logic. To support their accounts, appropriate theories of knowledge, language and the mind were developed, and further theories of morality, politics, aesthetics and religion came into being as the implications of the basic theory.

An alternative and more subjective approach to philosophy had, however, been developing since the work of Immanuel Kant, which placed emphasis on how we experience the world, rather than on the objective facts about it. This was combined with the idea of Marx that human consciousness is created by social conditions in ways of which we are hardly aware, and Nietzsche's desire to free ourselves from conventional morality in a quest to expand human possibilities.

This so-called Continental approach (because it emerged in Germany and then France) is now well-known in English-speaking countries, but few philosophers are well acquainted with both traditions. Both use technical terms, but Continental philosophers often create very personal concepts, and full understanding can only come from reading the original texts. For a long time the two traditions were not even on speaking terms, though greater attempts are now made to find common ground.

EDMUND HUSSERL (1859–1938)

The Continental tradition emerged with the development of phenomenology by Husserl. His starting point was that we need to focus on the exact nature of human experience before we can expand into an understanding of wider issues. The difficulty is that philosophers treat experience as interpreted by many theories, often in conflict with each other, and we are trapped into debates such as realism versus idealism, thus neglecting the nature of experience itself. Husserl's solution was to put nature and all its theoretical problems to one side by 'bracketing' them, which is not a denial of their importance, but a method of focusing on the neglected immediacy of consciousness. Phenomenology is not psychology (which offers explanations), but rather an attempt to properly confront raw experience, which is seen as the essential starting point for philosophy.

Having once bracketed the external world and its theoretical ideas, phenomenology attends closely to what is left, looking for the basis of our understanding, and our relationship to external reality. For example, Husserl considers the way we experience memories, and sees that they bring with them a direct sense of being in the past. When we encounter the minds of other people, we know them through facial and bodily expression, but also

Above: Husserl avoided the obscurities of idealism and metaphysics by focusing his new phenomenology on the nature of immediate experience.

recognize their inaccessibility to ourselves. Imagination carries with it a direct experience of being unreal. Consciousness is bound together by a Self or Ego, but this turns out (as Hume had said) to be very elusive as a phenomenon, and appears in different forms according to the experience involved.

Consciousness fluctuates, and so secure reports of it are hard to pin down. Husserl's solution was to look for the stable essence of each thing as it is encountered by imagining the properties of the thing being changed, and then seeing what must stay the same. If we can identify the stable essence of (say) a tree in this way, this gives us an 'idea' of the tree, extracted directly from experience, and the idea includes the category in which we place the tree. Husserl's aim was to build confidence in the external world by constructing it from indisputable experiences, but there is an inevitable idealism about his view. He could make no sense of any 'absolute reality' beyond experience, and so the only reality he could believe in had to be composed of ideas, even though he always believed that our ideas correlate with something outside of the mind.

This early account of phenomenology focused on the static essences of things, but Husserl later realized that thought is more dynamic, and so he introduced a 'genetic' account of the theory, focused on the processes and history which originate our ideas. He also broadened his approach to include other minds, which led to a phenomenological view of history.

MARTIN HEIDEGGER (1889–1976)

Heidegger began his career by interpreting Husserl's phenomenology more boldly. He saw the approach as answering ancient problems of metaphysics by giving us an account of ontology – the essential nature of existence. The question of Being had been neglected since the time of Parmenides and Plato, in favour of Aristotle's focus on the being of individual objects. Heidegger dismissed this as useful for science, but felt that phenomenology enables us to confront Being directly. Rather than trying to understand the being of objects, his key idea was to start with our own existence, which is far more obvious.

In his *Being and Time* of 1927 he took the German word *dasein* (being, or existence), and used it to mean existence as it is experienced by a human mind. Hence Dasein is the self-awareness of Being, and because each of us is Dasein, we each have an insight into Being in general. Given his starting point, Heidegger's findings from his phenomenology are rather different from Husserl's. He accepts the idea that we have no direct experience of an Ego, and that to presume such a thing would distort the phenomena we are trying to grasp. The two features of Dasein which are self-evident to us are that we have control over it, and that it is 'an issue' for us. That is, we face in-built conflicts about our own nature, its projects, and its choices.

For Heidegger, the traditional problems about knowledge, such as whether there is an external world and whether other minds really exist, fade away when we attend to the phenomena of experience. He disliked the concept of eternal and unchanging truth, because truth is historical and shifting. Sceptical problems about reality are empty questions, once we see how enmeshed our basic experience is within daily life. His famous example is our relationship to a hammer. We can give an objective description of a hammer, but the experience of a hammer is a direct contact with its powers and possibilities, especially when we pick it up. This 'ready-to-hand' experience reveals far more about the Being of Dasein than could ever be found in psychology or physics. Just as we experience the hammer, so we always experience qualities as 'of' something (so we experience red objects, but not 'redness'), and we experience values directly in the world (rather than the value-free world described by science).

So the dilemmas which face Dasein are not about existence, but about how to live. Other minds form a powerful community which puts pressure on individual Dasein, and threatens to dissolve it into the crowd. This creates a state of anxiety (*angst* – a concept Heidegger developed from Kierkegaard), and Dasein must claim itself back from this pressure. The dilemma is between the 'authenticity' of self-determination, and the inauthenticity when freedom is surrendered to others. The search for authenticity must navigate between three conflicting

Above: Heidegger developed a bolder form of Phenomenology, in which the nature of basic Being is revealed through private experience.

states of consciousness. We experience 'projection', which is a forward-looking awareness of possibilities and projects; but there is also the more passive experience of 'thrownness', which is the sense of being dropped into a reality which is not fully under our own control; and then there is 'fallenness', which is the sense of losing hold of one's own being. Thus our being is a battle for control of our own lives in an alien world that constantly threatens us. Our awareness of death plays a powerful role in focusing this struggle for authenticity, because we may be absorbed in the crowd but we die alone, and so the angst that arises from our knowledge of death forces us to take responsibility for our own free choices.

Being and Time is a founding work of the modern existentialist movement, especially because of its emphasis on anxiety and on making authentic choices, but Heidegger denied this after he changed his view considerably in the 1930s (after a period in which he actively supported the Nazi party). He doubted whether Being and Dasein can ever be explained, and his style of writing became more poetic. Rather than anxiety, he now saw the main human problem as a deep boredom, made worse by the increasing pressure on us of technological advances. Heidegger's influence was particularly strong in France, where he was taken to have dissolved the problems of metaphysics, and to have made our state of consciousness the central issue in philosophy.

JEAN-PAUL SARTRE (1905–80)

Like Heidegger, Sartre started from the phenomenology of Husserl. A key issue for phenomenologists is the existence or location of the Self within the phenomena of experience. The choices lie between the Self as a real part of experience, or as

Kant's hidden 'transcendental' Self which is implied by existence, or the sceptical empiricist view that if the Self is not experienced then we must reject it. Sartre opted for the third view, but his earliest work gave an account of why the Self remains important.

Sartre took consciousness as the starting point (and even proposed the slogan 'there is consciousness, therefore I am'), but he rejected idealist thinking, because without a real external world there can be no consciousness, which is always awareness *of* something. Consciousness is multi-layered, and can be seen as pre-reflective, reflective and self-reflective. Pre-reflective consciousness is simple awareness of the world, as when we focus on a bus as we race to catch it. Reflective consciousness thinks about the contents of the first layer, as when we think about buses, and the Self only appears at the third stage, when we consider ourselves as the thinker who is focused on buses. Hence we bring our Self into existence by an action of thought, but the external world has to be part of the thought, so the Self is not a private entity, but a part of the world.

In his *Being and Nothingness* of 1943, Sartre emphasized the way consciousness could be aware of absences, as when you observe that your friend is not in the café. This is a phenomenological experience of freedom, in which you see that things could be otherwise, and this absolute freedom of thought is what matters most. He distinguished Being 'in-itself' (external objects) from Being 'for-itself' (which is human experience). His modern view of Existentialism emerges from the idea that the mind is absolutely free, and that we create our own Ego, from which it follows that we can not only act freely but also remake ourselves. His slogan 'existence precedes essence' means that as long as we are alive we have no fixed essence or nature, because we are dominated by the fluctuations of phenomena and existence. Because Sartre believed that a person simply *is* their consciousness, he had no interest in the subconscious mind or psychoanalysis, because these are an evasion of the freedom which confronts us.

The challenge for existentialists is how to use our freedom. Sartre tells of a student faced during the war with the dilemma of fighting for his country or caring for his aged mother, and says there is no advice that can be given to this young man. When faced with such decisions we must aim for 'authenticity', which is fully facing up to our freedom of choice, recognizing all of the risks and consequences, and accepting responsibility. We must also face up to what we are, as well as what we choose, and Sartre says both cowards and heroes are responsible for their own characters. There are no excuses.

Above: Sartre led the popular Existentialist movement, focusing on the ability of individuals to remake themselves through their decisions.

The state to avoid is 'bad faith', which is a refusal to face such responsibility. Sartre famously illustrated the state of bad faith with the example of a waiter who hides behind his social role, and only accepts the responsibilities of a waiter, rather than of a human being. Authenticity is not the same as sincerity, because a waiter could be very sincere in his professional role, and yet not face up to his wider responsibilities. If a habitual gambler one day renounces their gambling, it turns out that one act of renunciation is not enough, because every day the temptation returns, and the freedom to resume the gambling never goes away. Existential 'anguish' can never be separated from this complete acceptance of freedom.

Sartre launched his Existentialism in 1945, and soon became immensely famous – 50,000 people attended his funeral in 1980. His later philosophy became less individualistic, and he searched for an existentialist approach to politics. Sartre's partner, Simone de Beauvoir (1908–86) applied existentialist thought to the situation of women, and famously observed that 'one is not born, but rather *becomes* a woman'. Thus Existentialism was the seed from which modern studies of gender emerged. But she also pointed out that an authentic acceptance of freedom was not of much use to a woman who lives in a harem, and that Existentialism needs a social and political dimension. We require the support of other people in order to build our own authentic self.

Sartre's attitude to other people was ambiguous. He wrote novels and plays which explored situations dominated by dilemmas and antagonism. In one play a character famously announces that 'hell is other people'. The only role other people have is to increase our self-awareness, as when someone feels shame because they have been caught spying through a keyhole. On the other hand, Sartre cared deeply about people who were oppressed. His political sympathies were Marxist and revolutionary, and he regularly led public demonstrations in support of disadvantaged groups. He gradually came to accept that freedom depends on 'situations', and is not just a private matter.

MICHEL FOUCAULT (1926–1984)

In the 1950s, the structuralist movement developed a view which rivalled phenomenology and existentialism. It challenged Sartre by arguing (like Marx) that consciousness is created by society rather than by each individual, and explained these social pressures in terms of language, the subconscious, mythology and sociology, which build up into social structures. Hence the individual self ceased to be of interest, and humanity could be explained socially.

Foucault shared these attitudes, but was also inspired by Nietzsche's view that what matters about truth is why it is valued and how it is used. Foucault never denied that the physical sciences are rational, but the human sciences such as psychology, economics and sociology were far from objective. He took seriously Nietzsche's interest in the 'genealogy' of knowledge and values, and so his work focused on the history of important social beliefs and attitudes. He understood thought in historical and social terms, rather than as an aspect of lone individuals. His response to Enlightenment optimism about reason was to investigate how such rationality responded to mental illness. Rather than increased sympathy, the response had been to exert power over such people, confining them in mental hospitals, and degrading them by a series of labels and theories.

Foucault came to understand social structures in terms of power, so that not only were dominant institutions developed, but modern human nature and individual personality (including emotions) were the creations of such power relations. As Sartre had said, the self is a creation of consciousness, but for Foucault consciousness is created by historical forces beyond the mind. This wasn't simply a matter of the strong oppressing the weak, as Marx had claimed. For Foucault, power structures are in every level of society, including family and sexual relationships, and hence politics is not just a matter of central government, but of relationships between people. Foucault thus pointed the way to new areas of study, such as 'sexual politics'. He noted, for example, the influence which regular confession to a priest in Roman Catholic churches had on people's attitudes to their own sexual feelings.

Power is so fundamental that Foucault had no revolutionary proposals for getting rid of it. On the contrary, power can be creative as well as oppressive, and the inevitable resistance to power is an important part of the picture. The evil aspect of power is 'domination', to which Foucault was certainly opposed, and his histories aimed to promote freedom (of both thought and life) by revealing the historical origins of domination. However, Foucault did not have a grand idea of full freedom for humanity, because there is no fixed human nature which needs liberating. He saw his books as tools for understanding beliefs, rather than as guides to action.

His next historical study was of the development of prisons, which focused on controlling and changing criminals (rather than on punishment), and his claim was that all modern institutions, such as schools, hospitals and factories, are based on the techniques invented for imprisonment. The architecture of prison design revealed how discipline was imposed on the

Above: Foucault's historical studies showed how life is best
understood as power relationships, even at the individual level.

prisoners, and new labels such as 'delinquent' and 'psychopath' slotted them into fixed categories (which allowed no ambiguities of gender, for example).

GILLES DELEUZE (1925-95)

Few philosophers have been as adventurous in their thinking as Gilles Deleuze. Like Foucault, he rejected structuralism, with its explanations based on static and impersonal linguistic structures. Deleuze had three philosophical heroes. Spinoza taught him the importance of immanence – meaning that everything is within nature, and there is nothing transcendent, such as a separate mind, or God. Nietzsche challenged us to answer the question 'How *could* we live?', rather than Socrates' question 'How *should* we live?', and taught us to actively affirm what we want from life. Henri Bergson (1859–1941) showed how important a subjective awareness of time is when we interpret human experience. Science presents time as precise intervals, with a vanished past and an unrealized future, but we experience the weight of the past, and expectations about the future, and the mind spreads time out for our inspection. From these three thinkers Deleuze developed views that focused on what is potential in nature, rather than on what is actual.

The three great traditions in ontology focus on pure Being (found in Parmenides and Heidegger), or on the being of objects (in Aristotle), or on Becoming and processes (in Heraclitus). Deleuze belongs to the third group, and he used the word 'difference' to express the unpredictability of existence, which can never be fully captured. His ontology focuses on the varied connections made as time passes, so that what we presume to exist continually changes. Even the traditional fixed categories of existence form for Deleuze a shifting pattern, and fail to capture aspects of nature that are not clearly individuated. Ontology is not a fiction or social convention, but a response to a changing world, and is described by Deleuze as a 'strange adventure'.

Deleuze modelled his metaphysics on biology, with a focus on living systems. The sequence old oak-acorn-new oak is not three objects but a single living system, and an egg is not just a potential creature but a living thing in its own right. He invited us to see as a model for Becoming a rhizome – an underground plant stem which extends roots in all directions, without a clear centre from which things branch. Different systems exhibit what he, writing with his colleague Félix Guattari (1930–92), called 'deterritorialization', illustrated by a wasp feeding on an orchid, where the two systems overlap and partially merge. Another favoured image was a 'body without organs', which is the concept we have of life in general, with its array of forces and potentials, of which we are part.

Deleuze was struck by the novel view of reality seen in modern cinema. Instead of the normal flow of phenomena, the cinema offers us short segments of experience, separated by sharp cuts, including flashbacks and sudden close-ups, and the audience copes easily with seeing reality in a quite new way. He invited us to see our lives as a series of 'lines', extending over time, like a group of connected stories. Some lines are 'rigid', when we just follow social conventions, and others are 'supple' when we take more control. His ideal is 'lines of flight', in which we achieve the freedom seen in the growth of the rhizome, and create a fresh vision of life.

He took the main activity of philosophy to be the creation of new concepts. He had no faith in the process of dialectical disagreements, because that traps us in conventional thought, and he suggested that new concepts might be hurled at people like stones from a medieval catapult. The main purpose of a new concept, he said, was to 'palpate' our conceptual scheme, the way a doctor might feel their way around a lump under the skin. In this way it is possible to open up new directions of thought. The main aim is not to find the truth, which is too elusive, but to reveal and make connections, and show us what is most interesting. Thought is not like analysis, but more like the state of mind of someone who is learning to swim.

His co-operation with Guattari led Deleuze to apply his vision to politics. He saw a connection between rigid older ontologies and liberal politics based on citizens as separate individuals. He agreed with Foucault that politics is part of the fine-grained details of ordinary life, rather than the headline events involving governments. To understand the concept of society you should understand the concept of a nomad, who lives a life free from our normal constraints. Because he wanted a more flexible attitude to subjective time, he was struck by the capitalist slogan that 'time is money', and saw this rigid capitalist attitude to time as the deepest problem of the modern world.

JACQUES DERRIDA (1930–2004)

Derrida is sometimes grouped with Foucault and Deleuze under the label of post-structuralism, but where Foucault studied history and Deleuze created concepts, Derrida chose to study the language of well-known texts in both philosophy and literature.

His starting point was the phenomenology of what happens when we use language. We have a rather static picture of spoken language, as words being neatly laid out in ordered structures, but the reality is very fluid, and (most importantly) a great deal of the activity is non-conscious.

Derrida accepted the idea that all consciousness is *about* something (it exhibits 'intentionality'), so that meaning is found in all of our experience, and not just in language. Hence the specific meanings of our words are displaced, being formulated unconsciously before the speech, and extending after its utterance. This makes the speaking of truth (and rational dialectic) effectively impossible, because the truth is in the elusive meaning, rather than in the words. If we aim for sincerity in speech (rather than truth) we encounter similar problems, because there is no way to verify whether any speech is sincere. Hence all language is an interweaving of fictions. He coined the word *différance* for this process by which language feels its way forward through continually distinguishing between extremes.

Spoken sentences are highly dependent on context and contain subtle ambiguities, and one sentence could even contradict itself (because someone could say 'I am ill' as a truth on one occasion, and then as a lie the next day). The use of proper names is particularly interesting. Analytic philosophers treat names as little more than logical labels, but the experience of using names is rich and complex, and Derrida suggests that the very idea that we have a Self is created by language, when we use the word 'I', or speak our own name. Language is also more metaphorical than we realize, and we should understand that metaphors are not just occasional techniques for description, but are basic to how language works.

Because speech is so fluid, with its meanings spread out over time, Derrida held the unusual view that the written word has priority over speech. In particular, philosophy needs static meanings which can be compared and repeated, and so he understood writing as the only medium in which any sort of metaphysics can be expressed. Speech involves the unconscious complexities of a speaker and a listener, but written language can contain meaning after the writer has died, or before the reader has started reading.

Even though written language is more persistent and stable, there still remains the problem of hermeneutics. This is the study of ways in which written texts are interpreted (which is especially important for historical scholars). A particular difficulty that arose is the hermeneutic circle – that each sentence is only understood in relation to the whole document, but the whole document depends for its understanding on each individual sentence. For Derrida, such problems even thwart our attempts to pin down meanings in written form. He observed that if you offer an interpretation of a text, you can also offer an interpretation of the interpretation, and there is no end to such a process. This means that traditional dreams of finding foundations for philosophy will always fail.

All of these awkward questions raised by Derrida are known as the deconstruction of a text. It led to Derrida having many critics, who accused him of denying truth, meaning, knowledge and reason, and thus appearing to preach the 'death of philosophy'. His image was not helped by his love of paradoxical remarks, and the wilful obscurity of his writing. Derrida, however, always denied such charges, and said he only deconstructed philosophical texts because he loved them so much. Like other French thinkers of his time, his aim was to disrupt conventional thought, and he revealed a picture of human experience which is much closer to the teachings of modern neuroscience than to the simpler pictures of previous generations.

CHAPTER 13

PHILOSOPHY SINCE 1960

In 360 BCE, philosophy was dominated by the figure of Plato. In the 1640s Descartes had similar prestige, and in the 1820s Hegel was the undisputed leader of the subject. In modern times it is unlikely that such a situation could recur, because of the vast range of modern thought and writing. Since 1945 the increased number and size of universities has transformed philosophical life. This has led to an increase in the number of talented thinkers, a high degree of specialization, the exploration of many new topics and higher standards of scholarship.

An obvious benefit of university expansion is the education of women, who have not only added fresh talent to the subject but have also introduced a new and influential point of view. In the Continental school the best-known women writers are Hannah Arendt (writing on political totalitarianism), Julia Kristeva, Hélène Cixous, Luce Irigaray and Judith Butler, and their work is notable for using techniques of deconstruction to reveal gender issues, both in classical texts and in discussions of contemporary problems. Important in the Analytic school are

Elizabeth Anscombe (who began the revival of virtue theory) and Martha Nussbaum, who developed new political thinking from her study of early Greek thought. In Miranda Fricker's *Epistemic Injustice* of 2007 the presumption of masculine authority about knowledge is laid bare, and in Kate Manne's *Down Girl* of 2017 analytical techniques are used to reveal the underlying attitudes in the hostility of many men to women.

Philosophy is a theoretical discipline, but it must respond to the facts of the real world. The ethics of warfare, for example, have been carefully reconsidered since the events of the two world wars. The sciences began slowly, and often took wrong turnings, but in modern times many secure and dramatic scientific findings have emerged which have greatly influenced philosophers. For example, the theory of evolution was slow to make an impact, but is now seen to affect our understanding of thought, morality and politics, as well as of biology. The concept of 'life' has at times had an almost mystical quality, but biochemistry (most famously with the discovery of DNA) has reduced life, at least in plants, to a chemical activity – which does not, of course, make life any less remarkable.

The Big Bang theory gives a clear framework in which to think about humanity, even if it leaves many puzzles unanswered. Cosmologists have discovered a new reason to believe in the existence of God, because the fundamental physical constants of the universe seem to be 'fine tuned' to the very special values needed to make human life possible – a fact for which physicists struggle to find a natural explanation. The puzzling nature of matter has now been revealed, down to a very low level of clearly identified particles and fields. The ultimate foundations may remain obscure, but when physicalist philosophers talk of the 'reduction' of something (such as the mind) to basic matter, they are now clear about what they mean.

Our modern ability to intervene in life or death issues has created many dilemmas, all of them needing clarity about underlying principles. Applied ethics is now a large new area of philosophy, with searches for guidelines to solve practical questions. When should a life-support machine be switched off? When should we divert funds from other deserving causes to pay for one expensive operation? When exactly does a human life begin or end? Should we intervene to 'design' the next generation? A related problem is the emergence of artificial intelligence, which confronts us with two major dilemmas. Should we try to make machines which enhance and improve the human body? Should we build machines which might actually replace us? If machines can take over a great deal of human activity, what is the remaining purpose of our lives?

In the writings of the Enlightenment, animals are routinely referred to as 'the brutes', and Descartes even viewed them as mere machines. The utilitarians introduced the idea that animals have moral significance because they can suffer. In recent years, research has revealed that many animals are vastly more intelligent than we believed, which changes their moral status, and their relationship to humanity. Who would have thought that crows can not only use tools, but can make them? Who would have thought that an octopus has brains in its tentacles? Certainly no one expected that a bonobo could use sign language to arrange a picnic with a group of human beings, and then toast a marshmallow in front of a fire. If we combine these revelations with our modern view of evolution, our integration into the animal world is becoming more obvious.

Developments in neuroscience have also greatly influenced philosophers. When surgeons divided the two halves of the brain in living patients to restrain the effects of epilepsy, it seemed to result in two persons living inside the same skull. The British philosopher Derek Parfit spotted the importance of this for our ideas of the Self and personal identity, and discussion has since been dominated by imaginative examples that challenge our instinctive assumptions. The mapping of brain activity has become increasingly fine-grained, and this has certainly encouraged a much more physical view of the mind, given that you can watch on a screen the brain activity that closely matches a pattern of thought.

Almost every area of human life involves a theoretical structure of concepts and principles, and can therefore be studied philosophically. When important areas are studied in this way, new forms of understanding are revealed. The philosophy of mathematics is a central study in Analytic philosophy, and there is great interest in the concepts of structures or patterns, and in what way numbers might be thought to exist. The philosophy of physics provides a focus on our concept of physical existence when it asks exactly what physicists mean by an object, a property, a force, an event, a law or energy. There are also flourishing philosophies of biology and chemistry which investigate the structures of life and matter and the emerging powers of a living cell, or of a molecule.

Continental philosophy has placed careful study of art and of human cultures at the heart of its thinking. Jean Baudrillard and Paul Virilio are both seen as philosophers, but most of their writings (influenced by Hegel, Marx and Freud) concern cultural influences on our beliefs and conscious experience. Baudrillard aimed to understand the bewildering influences on us of modern media, and Virilio wrote about the effect on our thinking of machines and warfare. The most notable books of the Marxist philosopher Theodor Adorno concerned music, and he saw the arts as a way of saving us from the drily objective world of science.

Analytic philosophers place a high value on logic, and so there is inevitably a flourishing philosophy of logic which studies concepts such as implication, proof, contradiction and truth. The study of logical 'models' has been a big area of growth, exploring the limits of our ability to create precise theories about the world. New systems of logic have appeared, and there is even a system of 'paraconsistent' logic in which contradictions are allowed (up to a point!).

Of course the end result of this development had to be the philosophy of philosophy, and this now exists. The history of philosophy shows a continual uncertainty about its own aims, ranging from Plato's belief that only philosophers can reveal reality to Locke's humble claim that he was just an 'under-labourer' for science. The 1991 book *What Is Philosophy?* of Deleuze and Guattari defended their creative view of the subject, while Timothy Williamson's *The Philosophy of Philosophy* (2007) argues the analytic case that only the most careful and precise analysis can lead to real progress.

MODERN REALITY

In philosophy the question of Being never goes away. In the first half of the twentieth century it was thought that such questions were either meaningless, or they could be ignored ('bracketed'). In the Continental tradition it is commonly held that metaphysics is now at an end, and Analytic philosophers have seen ontology as no more than a description of how we use words to discuss existence. In recent years there has been a strong challenge to this latter view. If we rely on science, that seems to rest on metaphysical assumptions, and it may be that every human being has a metaphysics, because we can't think about the world without a framework of basic beliefs.

Saul Kripke's *Naming and Necessity* of 1972 has been especially influential in this way. Kripke had previously shown how we can use the idea of possible worlds to interpret Modal Logic (concerning what is necessary or possible). If you say 'tigers might have been tame', or 'Aristotle might have been a musician', to what do 'tigers' or 'Aristotle' refer, if they are about possible tigers or possible Aristotle? Quine said that was so unclear that reasoning about possibilities cannot be done. Kripke said that the words refer to actual tigers and the actual Aristotle, and what the names refer to is kept consistent by their essential natures. Tigers are tigers and Aristotle was Aristotle because of their origin, and their essential physical character.

This sounds like merely technicalities, but it meant that tigers are necessarily a certain way, and that this essential nature is known by studying tigers. That is, some necessary truths can be discovered by empirical research. Since necessary truths are part of metaphysics, that means that metaphysics can be researched by scientists. Kripke's claim was controversial, but the result was a revival in metaphysics. Debates focused on whether objects have an 'essence', how names refer to things, and the modern concept of an object. Kripke's bold claim was that objects are obviously real, we refer to them directly (rather than via descriptions), and some of their properties can never change. Critics were not so sure.

The greatest sceptics were those who denied that our ontology contains 'objects'. We may accept the smallest particles of physics, but which collections of particles count as objects is just a matter of convention. If a ball breaks a window, it is the particles which do the work, so we don't need the 'ball' as an extra fact. Similarly, which features of an object count as 'essential' to it may always be a matter of opinion, depending on which aspects interest us. A new 'four-dimensionalist' view of objects was developed which understood objects as spread out across time, as well as across space. If an object is a collection of parts which is only agreed by convention, we can include the past and future parts if we want. We can then either treat an object as a fusion of its whole history (a space-time 'worm'), or treat it at any moment as just a 'time-slice' of something bigger. This seems to fit in with the space-time of special relativity and solve worries about the identity of an object from one day to the next.

David Lewis was an important thinker who pursued such ideas in his *On the Plurality of Worlds* of 1986. He was an empiricist who built his philosophy from a 'mosaic' of the smallest facts in our experience, and then extended them into possible worlds to build an account of causation, objects and laws of nature, thus providing a metaphysical background for science. Laws of nature are seen as the simplest possible descriptions of the patterns of events in the great mosaic, such as the law of gravity fitting every observed attraction between objects. Objects are four-dimensional, and everything else, such as the mind, is explained by reduction to the smallest facts (which are physical). Parts of Lewis' system are hard to accept, but its consistency is remarkable.

Medieval thinkers were divided between realists and nominalists, meaning that they thought properties such as squareness have their own independent existence, or else are merely names we employ for convenience. Modern nominalists are those who deny the existence of abstract objects, which includes properties, but mainly concerns numbers. Platonists such as Frege say that numbers are real objects, which exist independently of both the mind and the physical world. Frege's logicism (that numbers are among the eternal facts of logic) saw a revival in the 1980s, but it was met with hostility by those who asked how platonic numbers could possibly exist if they are outside the mind or the physical world, since they could then never make themselves known to us. The new rival view was fictionalism, which said that the numbers, and hence all the higher levels of mathematics, are simply invented by us, partly for convenience, and partly as an intellectual game.

MODERN KNOWLEDGE

A metaphysical theory needs not only an account of reality, but also an account of what we can know about that reality. This starts with an explanation of the concept of truth. There is now general agreement that the correspondence theory of truth (that thoughts are true when they precisely match their subject matter) cannot be defined clearly, and so realists are left with the view that truth is 'robust', but may be indefinable. More cautious views see truth as a mere verbal device for endorsing favoured sentences, and of no great importance. Other strategies are to measure truth by pragmatic success, or simply give rules for how the word 'true' can be used. A new and controversial idea is that every truth must have a 'truthmaker'.

In 1961, Edmund Gettier suggested that the traditional definition of knowledge as 'true justified belief' is incorrect, and he offered examples of well-supported beliefs which fail to be knowledge because of luck or misunderstanding. A lively debate about the nature of a successful justification soon followed. As a result, it is now sometimes claimed that knowledge is a useless concept and should be dropped, or that knowledge is not superior belief but rather that knowledge is normal (even in animals), and belief is just an inferior version. This externalist view says that justification is not further beliefs, but being correctly connected to the external facts.

More conventional views say that justification is either having coherent support for a belief, or good foundations for the belief (such as experience). Michel Foucault approached the problem by studying the 'archaeology' of knowledge, which explains knowledge through the history of how it was acquired by following a set of complex hidden cultural rules for 'discourse'. Similar views have appeared in analytic discussions as Contextualism, which says that what is acceptable as knowledge in one situation may be rejected in another.

A landmark in the philosophy of science was Thomas Kuhn's *The Structure of Scientific Revolutions* of 1962. His historical studies showed that the progress of science is not a smoothly developing response to a growing collection of observations. Instead, a 'paradigm' or theoretical framework is created, such as Newton's mechanics, and for a long period research is done within this 'normal' framework, with unusual observations being somehow fitted into the system. Eventually the system can't cope with problem cases, a sudden revolution occurs (a 'paradigm shift') and a new normal framework (such as relativity or quantum theory) is introduced. Kuhn's major point was that in a paradigm shift all the main vocabulary also changes its meaning, and so the new theory cannot be compared to the old one (the two being said to be 'incommensurable'). But if the words have changed, then the theories can't be compared, and progress cannot be assessed. The implication is that science changes but cannot be said to progress, which means we cannot talk about truth in science.

The relativism implied by Kuhn's book provoked a lot of opposition, and the aim since then has been to find alternative accounts of truth and progress in science.

Above: Thomas Kuhn provoked debates about science when he argued that its theories differed too much to be compared to one another.

Induction was already a problem, because repeated observations were supposed to reveal the truth, but empiricists said they revealed nothing more than our expectation of more similar observations. New problems surfaced for induction when it was realized that how you observe something depends on how you describe it, and that there are many ways to confirm something. Recent discussions have focused on the concept of a law of nature, which may actually be so idealized that it has no real application, or may not exist at all, apart from the features of the objects which obey the laws.

MODERN PERSONS

Analytic philosophers usually either believe that a person has a Self, or totally reject it. Continental philosophers since Kant have given much subtler accounts, often implying that we cannot help believing in a Self even when it is not real. Two interesting modern developments have added to the debate. The first is Parfit's response to the surgical division of a living brain, which led him to say that what matters about personal identity over time is not that some object called the Self survives, but that there is continuity of thinking. The test is what we care about, and we might not worry if the Self was divided in two, as long as the continuity of projects and memories is preserved.

The second idea arises from the externalist view of justification, which says that what matters for knowledge may be outside the mind. When it was suggested that the meanings of our words might also be outside our mind (in the physical world, or in society) this suggested the 'anti-individualist' view that the mind and the Self also extend beyond our own bodies (just as a modern mobile phone might be seen as an extension of its owner's mind).

The philosophy of mind has become a major area of study. Most older thinkers (apart from Spinoza) had assumed some sort of dualism, and treated the mind as very different from the body. The modern debate began when a group of Australian philosophers said that the mind simply *is* the brain and its activities. This led to the Physicalist view that either there is no mind (other than the brain), or that mental phenomena can all be explained physically. Traditional Cartesian dualists soon defended the idea that the mind is separate, but compromise theories also appeared.

Hilary Putnam's functionalist theory suggested that the mind is like the software running on the brain's hardware. This meant that the mind is not identical to the brain (as the physicalists suggested) because the software might be run on a different type of system (in principle, at least). The theory of emergentism, or property dualism, accepted that the mind is dependent on the brain, and thus part of a physical system, but held that it is also unique in acquiring its own causal powers, which are seen when we act for conscious reasons, rather than in a response to brain chemistry. This belief in the freedom of reason has been challenged by a finding in neuroscience that our actions seem to begin in brain activity which starts just before we become conscious of our own decisions.

The challenge from logical positivists that some ordinary language is actually unverifiable and therefore meaningless led to the philosophy of language as a major new area. The main aim was to find alternative theories of meaning, which were based either on truth or on the intention to communicate. More sceptical thinkers began to wonder whether so-called 'meanings'

are just imaginary, when all we have is words and ways of using them. The theory of how names and descriptive phrases refer to things in the world was also a major topic, not just because science needed it, but because language seems pointless if it doesn't somehow connect to reality.

MODERN SOCIETY

Modern ethical discussions have three levels. Meta-ethics deals with the fundamental status of values and moral truths; normative ethics seeks principles to guide correct behaviour; and applied ethics tries to resolve practical dilemmas. Meta-ethics is dominated by the question of whether there are moral facts – that is, are some features of morality just true, whether we like it or not, or is morality a human creation that leaves us free to choose our values?

Normative ethics was seen for a long time as a choice between the good intentions of Kant's deontology, or the good consequences of Utilitarianism. There have been two important modern developments. Dissatisfaction with both of those theories led to a revival of Greek virtue ethics, on the grounds that morality is about human character, rather than about performing correct actions. The second development was that Hobbes' contractarian ethics, which had always looked like a clever form of selfishness, were revived by the addition of mathematical game theory, which showed how self-interest can be combined with genuine concern for others. This modern approach is often supported by bioethics, which traces moral attitudes back to evolutionary strategies for survival and advantage. As we have seen, a major growth area has been in applied ethics, especially where modern medicine has created new dilemmas. Peter Singer pioneered this area, when he showed that utilitarianism implies important principles about animal rights.

Political theory has had to respond to dramatic practical events, particularly those involving communism or fascism. Marxism has adapted to the increasingly international character of capitalism. In France and Germany the main movement has been critical theory, which is a Marxist attempt to lay bare the way economic power affects every level of society and every human attitude. Jürgen Habermas has been notable for his theory of rational social communication, and he retains (contrary to most Marxists) some faith in the Enlightenment ideal of a rational political system.

In the English-speaking world the most important book is John Rawls' *A Theory of Justice* of 1971, which developed a new approach to liberalism. Rawls offered a rational defence of the welfare state by starting from the idea that everyone would want their society to have a social safety net if they thought that they themselves might need it. So he invited his readers to design a society of which they would be a member, on the blindfold assumption (from behind the 'veil of ignorance') that their place in the society was not yet known – so the reader might be rich or poor, healthy or disabled, young or old, male or female. He claimed that in such circumstances we would be most concerned about the fate of the least well off. Hence that should be the priority of a rational liberal society (in which all citizens have roughly equal importance). The book went on to develop an account of the requirements of this basic safety net. Most conservative responses to this book have emphasized the importance of the free market, and the injustice of high taxation.

The key issues in modern political debate are freedom and equality. Notable among liberal thinkers is the American philosopher Martha Nussbaum, who has expanded the idea that a good society should enable every citizen to fulfil their capabilities, even if that needs help from the state. In France, the pursuit of freedom has been central to philosophy since the rise of Existentialism, and all of the leading thinkers have looked for ways to free our thinking from cultural pressures in order to make way for a truly free society. Most liberal discussion has focused on the types of freedom which are needed (such as thought, speech, health care, education, suitable taxation, housing) in order to avoid authoritarian societies from either the right or the left.

Above: John Rawls re-launched political philosophy with his theory of how we can achieve justice in a liberal society.

Possibly the liveliest debate in all of Western culture (and not just in philosophy) concerns equality. Every Western country is now a democracy, but they all contain marginalized groups who lack the power to participate. Hence a great deal of political philosophy now concerns equal rights for all genders (including those who are transgender), all religious faiths, children, and all sexual orientations. The values which drive these discussions are often found in Enlightenment thinkers, and so the application of those earlier ideas to our current concerns is common in current writings.

LOOKING BACK

If there is one thing we should learn from the history of philosophy, it is respect for our ancestors. It is tempting to look down on people of the past because their knowledge and technology were more limited than our own, but their surviving philosophical writings quickly show that this attitude is entirely wrong. The facts of the human world have changed a great deal, but the fundamental problems of human existence remain very similar to those which faced Socrates. These writings are not just impressive for their time. There are many topics in philosophy about which the best discussion we have was written two thousand years ago. Each generation of thinkers responds to the thoughts of the previous generation, but philosophers also respond to much earlier works, and those books are our most important resource for learning how to think well.

What matters about these writings is the challenge they offer. In ordinary life we give little thought to how much we take for granted about ourselves, our values, our knowledge and our language. Philosophers have taught us that we cannot think clearly about anything if we have not given some thought to these prior assumptions. The history of philosophy is an unveiling of layer after layer of unquestioned beliefs, and the gradual creation of tools and techniques that can be used to challenge them. But to challenge a belief is not to reject it, and our aim is to find beliefs which can survive such criticism. In the end what matters is not which thinker is the most exciting or dazzlingly brilliant, but which of them is right.

A TIMELINE OF WESTERN PHILOSOPHY

(SOME DATES ARE APPROXIMATE)

585 BCE	Thales theorizes that water is the fundamental substance of nature.
570 BCE	Anaximander suggests the *apeiron* as the fundamental substance.
550 BCE	Anaximenes probably wrote the first philosophy book.
530 BCE	Pythagoras proposes that nature is basically mathematical.
490 BCE	Heraclitus flourishes in Ephesus.
470 BCE	Parmenides and Zeno of Elea flourish on the Italian coast.
460 BCE	Anaxagoras says mind is an essential part of reality.
455 BCE	Empedocles develops the idea of four essential elements – earth, air, fire and water.
430 BCE	The Sophists, such as Gorgias and Protagoras, flourish in Athens.
420 BCE	Democritus develops his physicalist and atomist theory.
415 BCE	Socrates becomes famous for his public discussions in Athens.
399 BCE	Trial and execution of Socrates.
387 BCE	Plato founds the Academy in Athens.
380 BCE	Plato's *The Republic*.
360 BCE	Diogenes of Sinope argues for the simplest possible life.
335 BCE	Aristotle founds the Lyceum and writes his main works.
325 BCE	Pyrrho of Elis argues that humans know almost nothing.
306 BCE	Epicurus founds a school called The Garden in Athens.
301 BCE	The Stoic school is founded in Athens by Zeno of Citium.
230 BCE	Chrysippus becomes the head of the Stoic school.
87 BCE	The Athenian schools are closed by the Roman Army.
60 BCE	Lucretius writes his long Epicurean poem *On the Nature of Things*.
45 BCE	The retired Roman statesman Cicero writes many works on philosophy.
60 CE	Seneca writes his stoic essays and letters in Rome.
95 CE	The slave Epictetus writes his stoic *Discourses*.

160   The Roman Emperor Marcus Aurelius writes his stoic *Meditations*.

180   Sextus Empiricus writes several works defending sceptical philosophy.

250   Diogenes Laertius writes his *Lives of the Eminent Philosophers*.

270   Porphyry compiles Plotinus' Neo-Platonist work *The Enneads*.

427   St Augustine of Hippo's *The City of God*.

524   Boethius' *The Consolation of Philosophy*.

529   Justinian I permanently closes the ancient philosophical schools.

1027   Ibn Sina published *The Healing*.

1078   Anselm of Canterbury sets out the Ontological Argument for the existence of God.

1111   Abu Hamid al-Ghazzali's *The Incoherence of the Philosophers*.

1140   Peter Abelard is accused of heresy.

1170   Ibn Rushd writes a series of commentaries on Aristotle.

1274   Aquinas completes his *Summa Theologica*.

1305   John Duns Scotus lectures in Paris.

1320   William of Ockham lectures in Oxford.

1417   Re-discovery of Lucretius' *On the Nature of Things*.

1513   Niccolò Machiavelli's *The Prince*.

1543   Andreas Vesalius' *On the Fabric of the Human Body*.

1543   Nicolaus Copernicus' *On the Revolutions of the Celestial Spheres*.

1569   Michel de Montaigne's *Essays*.

1605   Francis Bacon's *The Advancement of Learning*.

1637   René Descartes' *Discourse on the Method*.

1641   Descartes' *Meditations*.

1651   Thomas Hobbes' *Leviathan*.

1677   The *Ethics* of Spinoza is published.

1687   Isaac Newton's theory of gravity appears in *Principia Mathematica*.

1689   John Locke's *Two Treatises of Government*.

1690   Locke's *An Essay Concerning Human Understanding*.

1713   George Berkeley's *Three Dialogues between Hylas and Philonous*.

1715   Gottfried Leibniz's *Monadology*.

1739   David Hume's *A Treatise of Human Nature*.

1762 Jean-Jacques Rousseau's *The Social Contract.*

1781 Immanuel Kant's *The Critique of Pure Reason.*

1785 Friedrich Jacobi's *Letters on the Teachings of Spinoza.*

1786 Karl Reinhold's *Letters on the Kantian Philosophy.*

1789 Jeremy Bentham's *Introduction to the Principles of Morals and Legislation.*

1789 The French Revolution begins in Paris.

1792 Mary Wollstonecraft's *A Vindication of the Rights of Women.*

1794 Johann Fichte's *Science of Knowing.*

1795 Novalis and Friedrich Schiller lead the new Romantic Movement.

1799 Friedrich Schelling's *Philosophy of Nature.*

1807 Georg Hegel's *The Phenomenology of Spirit.*

1816 Georg Hegel's *The Science of Logic.*

1819 Arthur Schopenhauer's *The World as Will and Representation.*

1830 Auguste Comte's *Introduction to Positive Philosophy.*

1841 Ludwig Feuerbach's *The Essence of Christianity.*

1843 Søren Kierkegaard's *Fear and Trembling* and *Either/Or.*

1848 Karl Marx and Friedrich Engels write *The Communist Manifesto.*

1861 John Stuart Mill's *On Liberty,* and *Utilitarianism.*

1867 Karl Marx's *Capital vol. 1.*

1877 Charles Sanders Pierce's 'The Fixation of Belief' launches Pragmatism.

1884 Gottlob Frege's *Groundwork of Arithmetic,* using his new logic.

1886 Friedrich Nietzsche's *Beyond Good and Evil.*

1897 Georg Cantor begins Set Theory, and reveals new mathematical infinities.

1903 G.E.Moore's *Principia Ethica* attacks Utilitarianism.

1903 Bertrand Russell's *The Principles of Mathematics.*

1918 C I Lewis creates Modal Logic.

1896 Henri Bergson's *Matter and Memory.*

1913 Edmund Husserl's *Ideas: General Introduction to Pure Phenomenology.*

1921 Ludwig Wittgenstein's *Tractatus Logico-Philosophicus.*

1926 Logical positivism is developed in Vienna by Carnap, Schlick and Neurath.

1927 Martin Heidegger's *Being and Time.*

1930 Kurt Gödel's Incompleteness Theorems prove the limitations of arithmetic.

1943 Jean-Paul Sartre's *Being and Nothingness*, which launches modern Existentialism.

1944 Adorno and Horkheimer's *Dialectic of Enlightenment*.

1949 Gilbert Ryle's *The Concept of Mind*.

1952 Simone de Beauvoir's *The Second Sex*.

1950s Structuralism in linguistics and sociology is developed.

1951 Hannah Arendt's *The Origins of Totalitarianism*.

1953 Ludwig Wittgenstein's *Philosophical Investigations* are published.

1956 U.T. Place and J.J.C.Smart propose a wholly physical view of the mind.

1958 Elizabeth Anscombe begins the revival of virtue theory.

1960 Willard Quine's *Word and Object*, showing the limitations of language.

1962 Thomas Kuhn's *The Structure of Scientific Revolutions*.

1963 Edmund Gettier challenges the traditional definition of knowledge.

1967 Hilary Putnam proposes his Functionalist theory of the mind.

1967 Jacques Derrida's *Of Grammatology*.

1968 Gilles Deleuze's *Difference and Repetition*.

1970 Saul Kripke gives his *Naming and Necessity* lectures.

1971 Derek Parfit argues that brain surgery can prove that personal identity is not important.

1972 John Rawls gives a new account of liberalism in *A Theory of Justice*.

1975 Hilary Putnam proposes that meaning in language is partly outside the mind.

1975 Michel Foucault's *Discipline and Punish*.

1975 Peter Singer's *Animal Liberation*.

1975 Jerry Fodor argues that the mind has modules with their own internal language.

1986 David Lewis' *On the Plurality of Worlds*.

1991 Deleuze and Guattari write *What is Philosophy?*

2007 Miranda Fricker's *Epistemic Injustice*.

2007 Tim Williamson's *The Philosophy of Philosophy*.

2010 Martha Nussbaum's *Creating Capabilities*.

2018 Kate Manne's *Down Girl*.

INDEX

PICTURE CREDITS